Christianity,

Where Can This Path Take Me?

Dedication:
To the people of St. Croix,
United States Virgin Islands
2019
KLS

Remember that every book, recording, magazine or article ever written about the Bible or Christianity is filtered through the author's life. These are not scripture or authoritative. The only way to really know for yourself what God wants for your life is to read the Source, the Bible, yourself. I hope this volume gets you started in your own personal quest.

Equipment Check

✓ Correct Map
✓ Compass that points to True North.

The Appalachian Trail is a 2,180+ mile long public trail that traverses the scenic, wooded, pastoral, wild of the Appalachian Mountains (bears, snakes and rough terrain included). You would not think of beginning this long trek without the proper equipment. The Christian trek is no different. You need the correct map, an internationally accepted, easily read, translation of the Bible. You also need your compass set on who will be directing your journey, Christ Jesus, Himself through His Holy Spirit.

In order to begin this track, you need to understand the premise of the journey: Christianity. It is as obvious today as it was in the first century when Paul wrote most of the New Testament that there are some who take on the name but do not, in any way, represent what Christianity really is (Titus 1:16). These people muddy the water for those interested in knowing what Christianity can mean for their personal lives. The only way to really know what Christianity is and what Christ wants to mean personally to you, in your life, and from right now where you are in life is to read the Bible yourself and find out for yourself. This work provides a guided method for that discovery.

The first and foundational concept must be that your map, the Bible, is truthful and can apply to your life right now. Although the Bible was written down over centuries by many people remember it had only one inspiration – the Holy Spirit. A Christian's concept of the inerrancy of scripture applies to the original autographs (manuscripts). Inerrancy does not extend to every copy and translation that was created from those original manuscripts. People often misunderstand this concept of inerrancy. When someone has discovered what they consider to be an error in one of the translations they could assume that the Bible as a whole must contain errors. In truth, the difference probably resulted from a translation committee decision on how to translate a passage from the original manuscript. The original text, especially the Greek language, is very expressive. Greek and Hebrew can be hard to translate into English. For example, the English word "love" has several words in Greek with varied meanings. Hebrew can also express more in a word than what can be easily translated into an English word.

The second foundational concept must be that God, through Jesus Christ and the Holy Spirit, loves you personally. He has a plan for your life if you will accept it. God's love has a gift for you if you accept it. The Gift is that God sent His only Son to be sacrificed as the legal penalty to save you from eternal separation from Him. God loves you enough to offer that Gift to you, but He also loves you enough to allow you to make your own choice on accepting this Gift. If you do not accept it, He will allow your choice to stand and you will remain separated from His love and from His plan for your life here on earth and you will be eternally separated from Him at death. God does not "send" anyone to Hell. Hell was created for Satan and the fallen angels. People can, though, chose Hell instead of Heaven. Christ wants to be your compass for this life journey.

The third foundational concept is that no one can make that decision to accept or reject God's Gift for you. Not making a decision, or putting it off, is a rejection on your part. Joining a church, organization, religious group, being baptized, saying spiritual things, "turning over a new leaf," being as good as you can be, not doing something really bad (in your opinion) – none of these things get you even close to a personal relationship with God.

Christianity is not an add-on to your life. World religions have multiple gods to choose from. Christianity is not something you add on to Buddha, Mohamed, some prophet or good deeds. It is a single life experience which stands by itself and accepts no other ideology in your life. You must know what Christ did on the Cross yourself. You must accept that sacrifice He made for you, yourself. You must ask Him to forgive you of your past sin (rebellion) and ask Him to come into your life and make you a new person. Only YOU can do that.

Every Christian has a "testimony" about what they were before, how they accepted Christ into their life, and what has changed in their life since the moment they accepted Christ's sacrifice for their personal sin (being "born again"). Someone else's testimony will not save you; it only confirms that others have been where you are right now. Some testimonies are large involving gross habits and lifestyles that these people were freed from. Other testimonies are simple. Everyone, though, would agree that who they were before accepting Christ's sacrifice for their sin is not who they are anymore. That change is a promise from God to you. You don't have to go on living in shame, heartache, hate, separation, frustration or loss. Christians are a community. We aren't perfect and we can and will make mistakes, but the focus of our lives is on what is ahead not dwelling on what happened before.

There are a couple of illustrations in this book of what we can call 'The Plan of Salvation' for you to read. They are shown on pages 63-67. In addition, William Fay in his book <u>Share Jesus Without Fear</u> (B&H Publishing Group, Nashville, 1999) lists the following scripture references from the NIV translation of the Bible. It is important to read each of them out loud and ask yourself after each reference, "What does this say to me?":

Romans 3:23 "For all have sinned and fall short of the glory of God."

Romans 6:23 "For the wages of sin is death, but the gift of God is eternal life in Christ Jesus our Lord."

John 3:3 "In reply Jesus declared, 'I tell you the truth, unless a man is born again, he cannot see the kingdom of God."

John 14:6 "Jesus answered, 'I am the way and the truth and the life. No one comes to the Father except through me.'"

Romans 10:9-11 "That if you confess with your mouth, 'Jesus is Lord,' and believe in your heart that God raised him from the dead, you will be saved. For it is with your heart that you believe and are justified, and it is with your mouth that you confess and are saved. As the Scripture says, 'Anyone who trusts in him will never be put to shame.'"

2 Corinthians 5;15 "And he died for all, that those who live should no longer live for themselves but for him who died for them and was raised again."

Revelation 3:20 "'Here I am! I stand at the door and knock. If anyone hears my voice and opens the door, I will come in and eat with him, and he with me.'"

Now it is decision time. You can never again say you do not know these facts. What is your choice right now, right here? Read through pages 143-146 for more and a guided prayer.

Be diligent to present yourself approved to God as a workman who does not need to be ashamed, accurately handling the word of truth.

2 Timothy 2:15,
Ryrie Study Bible NAS

This book is a combination of original thoughts as well as works in the public domain and references to copyrighted materials. It is a resource for people searching for answers. This includes new believers or those wanting to move forward with their life in Christ. As the compiler, I encourage you to make the effort to change. You had an old life before becoming a Christian. Now you can live a new life of more fulfillment and joy as you walk along the path of life. Read. Study. Live.

A companion book in this <u>Christianity,</u> series* provides a topical index. While not exhaustive it is useful for Bible study, instruction and general answers to some of life's questions.

Bible study methods: Try different study methods to bring out the depth of understanding available to you from the Bible. There are several different options for reading through the Bible

---

* Christianity, Bible References by Topic

noted later in this book. There are many more available online. You can begin those at any date and read through as noted until you have come back to your starting date. You do not have to wait to start on January 1st. It is a good idea to read through the entire Bible so you can grasp the picture and substance of the Book.

In the spiritual exercise of reading and studying Scripture, it is important to let God speak to you. The quantity of material you read today is not as important as the quality of what you get out of those verses. Even a person who does not consider themselves to be a "Christian" can ask God to speak to them through the Bible. After reading a passage ask the Holy Spirit to help you see what you need from that passage for that very day. Re-read the passage if necessary, to grasp the meaning. Ask yourself questions about what you have read such as:

- ✓ Does this tell me anything about God or Christ or the Holy Spirit? If so, what?
- ✓ Does this tell me anything about myself and how I should live? If so, what?
- ✓ Does this tell me anything about other people and my responsibilities to, or relationships with them? If so, what?

Keep a journal of your studies and of your prayers. Write down what this passage meant to you today and your prayer requests to God about today's reading. This will help you to recognize answered prayers in the future. It will help you to see how you have grown in your knowledge and understanding of Christ in the years to come.   *KLS*

Journal   Date:

Scripture Read:

What this scripture means to me:

Prayer Requests:

Prayer Praise:

Prayer Answered:

FREQUENTLY ASKED QUESTIONS

These topical studies came about during a Baptist Student Union student leadership bible study in the early 1970s under the direction of Dr. Max Barnett at the University of Oklahoma, Norman, OK. They were meant to address questions by college students regarding Christianity. Additional comments, references, or clarifications have been added here to the basic study outlines for clarity. Additional resources are available through this link:

https://swbts.edu/academics/faculty/church-family-ministries/max-barnett/

Receiving God's Forgiveness

I. What is God's Forgiveness?

  a. Blood-bought atonement (Heb 9:22; Lev 5:4-10; Matt 26:28; Titus 2:13-14; Rev 1:5) Atonement is satisfaction of a legal penalty.

  b. God's total forgetting of our sin (Ps 103:12; Micah 7:19; Matt 26:28) Remission is a term used to refer to cancer or leukemia which has been healed. It means that now such complete healing has occurred that it appears as though it never existed.

  c. Justification (Acts 13:38-39) A judicial decision made by God at a Christian's conversion that although we are not blameless, from now on He considers us blameless because all He sees when He looks at us is the blood of Christ which covered our old sin once we accepted Christ into our lives.

  d. Our becoming the righteousness of God (2 Cor 5:21) Becoming a Christian means that all that God is, comes to dwell in us through the presence of the Holy Spirit.

II. Why We Need God's Forgiveness

  a. The Non-Christian

    i. As an eternal creation of God, we are marked for doom without it (John 3:36; Jer 2:22; 5:25; Ezra 9:15)

    ii. There is no other means of justification / salvation because through Christ alone we are brought into right relationship with God (Acts 13:38-39; John 14:6; Acts 4:12; I Peter 3:18; Heb 10:26)

    iii. God longs to forgive us (Isa 1:18; 43:25-26)

    iv. Because we need a new nature (Eph 2:1-10)

b. The Christian

    i. It is necessary to receive God's blessings (Rom 4:7-8; Ps 32:1-2)

    ii. It enhances the reputation of God (Ps 79:9)

    iii. It produces reverence for God (Ps 130:4; Luke 7:47)

    iv. To remove guilt (Heb 10:2,17-18; Col 2:13-14)

    v. Brings freedom to experience God's purpose for us which is to live, not for ourselves, but for him (2 Cor 5:9,21; Phil 1:21)

    vi. Because we still sin by yielding to our old nature (Rom 6:10-12; Rom 7:19-20)

    vii. To have an effective prayer life (Ps 66:18; Isa 59:1-2; John 15:7-8)

    viii. To have a powerful life (2 Chron 16:9a)

    ix. It is essential to avoid living a defeated life (1 Kings 8:33-34; Ps 32:1)

III. How to Receive God's Forgiveness

a. The Non-Christian
   i. Believe in Jesus through faith in His blood sacrifice
      for you (Acts 10:43; Mark 2:5; Matt 26:28; Heb 10:14)

b. The Christian

   i. Confess

      1. Search your heart for sin (Ps 139:23-24; Ps 19:12)

      2. Allow God to convict you – visualize what you
         have done to God's heart because of your sin
         (Ps 51:3-4; Gen 39:9)

      3. Ask God's forgiveness for each specific sin
         (1 John 1:9; Ps 32:5; Prov 28:13)

      4. Trust God for forgiveness on the basis of His
         loving, merciful character (Ps 51:1-2; Mark 2:7;
         Lam 3:22-23; Ps 78:38; 2 Chron 7:14)

   ii. Repent – change the direction of your life in the area
       of sin (Ps 51:10; 2 Cor 7:8-10)

   iii. Forgive others (Matt 6:14-15; Luke 6:37)

In order to know what we need to confess; it is essential to
understand how the Scriptures define sin.

Sin is:

      1. Doing what God says not to do (Ex 20:1-17)
      2. Not doing what we know is right to do
         (James 4:17)

3. Doing anything from a motive other than faith (Rom 14:23)
4. Doing something that causes a brother or sister to stumble (Rom 14:21)

Once you ask for forgiveness with a true heart of repentance, God promises that the sin is forgiven and thus forgotten. Many times, our nature will accuse us and bring that forgiven sin back to mind. Claim God's forgiveness to yourself. Memorize 1 John 1:9 and stop allowing the past to accuse you any further. Sin sometimes is a momentary thing that happened, other times though it is the manner of life you have lived and just like the path cattle will follow through the field, you have made a rut to walk in. Ask God to help you get out of that sin-rut and make every change necessary to not put yourself in a place of temptation and go down that old rut ever again. If you fail, ask forgiveness again and learn from that mistake where you are vulnerable and make any life changes necessary. See Clear Conscience that is included in this list of studies.

How Can I Have Assurance of My Salvation And Eternal Life?

I. What is Assurance of Salvation?
   a. A conviction that we know God (2 Tim 1:12)
   b. Realizing you have entered an unbreakable <u>relationship</u> with God, instead of just a breakable <u>fellowship</u> (John 1:12-13; Ps 37:23-24)
   c. Realizing God is responsible for keeping our imperishable salvation for us (1 Peter 1:3-5; 1 Cor 1:8-9; Jude 24-25; John 10:27-30)
   d. It is God's Spirit bearing witness to our spirit that we are children of God (Rom 8:9,16; 2 Cor 13:5; 1 John 4;13-15)
   e. Believing God's promises (Rom 10:9-13; John 3:16; 5:24; Heb 6:17-20)
       Salvation is a gift (Eph 2:8-9)
       His gifts are irrevocable (Rom 11:29)

II. Why Do We Need Assurance of Salvation?
   a. Assurance is commanded in order to have a true heart before God (Heb 10:19-23)
   b. Assurance is necessary in order to love your brothers and sisters in Christ (1 John 3:14,18; 4:18-19; John 13:34-35)
   c. Assurance is necessary for victory over Satan (Eph 6:10-17…particularly the helmet of salvation)
   d. Assurance is necessary to give us confidence and boldness (Heb 10:19; 2 Tim 1:7)

III. How Can We Have Assurance of Salvation?

    a. Examine your life in light of the evidence of conversion (1 John 2:5b,6)

        1. Awareness of - turning from sin (1 Thess 1:8-10)
        2. Hunger for God's Word (1 Peter 2:2)
        3. Desire for a changed life (2 Cor 5:17; Isa 26:9)
        4. Increase in testing (2 Tim 3:12)
        5. A love for other Christians (John 13:34-35)
        6. Desire to share Christ that others may know Him (Ps 107:2; Jer 20:9; 1 Cor 9:16,17; 1 Thess 1:8-10)
        7. The Holy Spirit has entered your life (Rom 8:9)
        8. You confess and believe that Jesus has come in the flesh (1 John 4:1-3)
        9. You confess and believe that Jesus is the Son of God (1 John 4:15; 5:1)
        10. You confess and believe that Jesus Christ is Lord (1 Cor 12:3)

    b. If these are true, believe God that you will always be a Christian (Eph 3:12)

    c. Live an obedient life (1 John 3:21-23; Isa 32:17)

    d. Be diligent and minister to others (Heb 6:10-11; 2 Cor 3:5-6)

IV. Passages often misunderstood when studying assurance:

    a. Heb 6:4-8 Often interpreted as teaching you can lose your salvation having once had it:

        1. In verses 4-6 the writer teaches that if a person could lose his salvation, it would be impossible for him to be saved again because Jesus would have to

be born of a virgin, live a perfect life, and die on the cross again in order for us to be saved again (Heb 6:4-6; 10:10-18). Jesus is not going to do that (1 Peter 3:18; Heb 9:25-28; 10:10-18). So, this passage does not teach that salvation can be lost but merely that if it could be lost, it could not be restored.

2. In verses 7 and 8, it is clear that it is not the person who became a Christian and then fell back into evil works that is going to burn, but it is his works, the fruit of the land, which will be destroyed. The person is only near to being cursed and will be saved, though his works will be consumed (1 Cor 3:15).

b. Heb 10:26-27 Often interpreted that our deliberately sinning after our conversion causes us to lose our salvation but:

Again, the context clearly indicates a reference to the all-sufficient one-time sacrifice which God made in Christ and if we look for another sacrifice to provide a way of salvation, we will be disappointed, for there never will be another (Heb 9:25-28; 10:10-18,28,29; 1 Peter 3:18). God does not allow us to set aside the sacrifice of His Son without severe punishment (Heb 10:28).

c. 2 Peter 2:9-22 Often interpreted as teaching that a Christian falling back into the ways of the world loses his salvation and is worse off than he was before becoming a Christian, but:

1. It is clear from this passage that those who are deceived are those who barely escape eternal punishment (2 Peter 2:18,20). They have escaped eternal punishment but do not live abundant lives because they were deceived.

2. The Greek word "if" at the beginning of verse 20 is a third-class condition of the word and should be literally translated *"if (but it is impossible for it to happen)."* So, from the very choice of Greek words, the writer shows that it is impossible to escape the defilements of the world and then become so entangled in them again as to be overcome by them and so lose salvation.

d. Galatians 5:4   Often interpreted as teaching the "falling from grace" means losing salvation but reading Galatians chapters 3 through 5 makes it clear that Paul is referring not to losing salvation but to falling back into bondage to the law (do this, don't do that) rather than accepting justification before God as a free gift through faith.

How Can I Have Fellowship (a relationship) With God?

Daily fellowship with God is necessary in order to allow God to give you constant cleaning from sin as well as refreshment and guidance.

I. What is fellowship with God?

   a. Becoming one with God through partaking of His divine nature (2 Peter 1:4; Rom 12:2; John 17:20-21; 1 John 2:5-6)
   b. Allowing God to talk and explain scripture to us (Luke 24:32; 1 Jn 2:27; Ps 27:11; 32:8)
   c. Gaining an intimate knowledge of Christ (Phil 3:10)
   d. Because He wants to talk to us (Ex 34:1-3; Jer 33:3; Heb 1:1-2)
   e. Because we need to talk to Him (James 1:5; Heb 4:16; 1 Chron 16:11; 2 Tim 3:16-17; Phil 4:6-7)
   f. An attitude of seeking God instead of performing activities (Ps 27:4,8; Ps 42:1-2; 63:1; Hos 6:6; 1 Sam 15:22; Ps 51:16-17)

II. Why do we need fellowship with God:
   a. We have been called to fellowship (1 Cor 1:9)
   b. The Holy Spirit within us cries out for fellowship (Gal 4:6)
   c. We cannot bear fruit without fellowship (John 15:4-5)

d. Because we have been joined with Christ (2 Pet 1: 4-20; Gal 4:7; Eph 2:1-3; Rom 8:9)

e. Because God loves us as much as He loves Jesus (1 Jn 4:9-10; John 3:16; 15:9-11; 17:22-23; Jer 29:11-13)

f. God desires and seeks our fellowship (John 14:23; John 4:23-24)

g. God alone is the answer to our deepest longings (Ps 73:25; Rev 21:4; 1 Cor 10:13)

h. It is necessary for guidance (Ps 32:8; Jer 29:11; Jn 14:26; Isa 58:11)

i. It is necessary for confidence and to not be ashamed at Christ's return (1 John 2:28; Mark 8:38)

III. How to have fellowship with God

a. Become a Christian (John 14:6; Rev 3:20; Jn 1:12; Acts 2:38; 1 Jn 1:9; Eph 2:8-9)

b. Separate yourself from sin (2 Cor 6:16-18; 2 Chron 16:9a: Ps 24:3-5; 66:18; 1 John 3:6)

c. Approach God with praise and humility (Ps 100:4; 61:8; Ex 15:2; Isa 57:15; 66:2)

d. Ask God to give you a longing heart for fellowship with Him (Ps 63:1; Ps 17; Hosea 6:3; James 4:8)

e. Let God talk to you and be involved in His Word (Acts 17:11; Luke 24:27,32; 2 Tim 3:16-17; Rom 10:17; Ps 119:105)

f. Pour out your feelings and desires to God (Ps 62:8)

g. Obey (John 14:21-23; 15:10,14; 1 John 3:24)

h. Walk in the light (Ps 119:105; Eph 5:8-11; John 8:12; 1 John 1:5-7; 4:20,21; Prov 6:23; James 5:16) It is necessary to be open and transparent with others, confessing your sin to them when we have hurt them and asking forgiveness.

i. Walk as Jesus walked (1 John 2:5-6). We must have on our heart what Jesus had on his heart to really fellowship with Him. What was on Jesus' heart was loving God and reaching people (John 4:34-38).

IV. Lifelong results of fellowship with God

a. Grace and peace multiplied (2 Peter 1:2)

b. Granted everything pertaining to life and godliness, partaking of the Divine nature (2 Peter 1:3-4)

c. Escape from corruption in the world (2 Peter 1:4b; 1 John 5:4)

d. Personal instruction and council (2 Tim 3:16; Ps 32:8)

e. Ability to abide (live) in Him (John 15:3-5; 1 John 2:24,28)

f. Insight from the Bible (James 2:5; Josh 1:8; Deut 17:19)

g. God becomes your refuge (Ps 62:8; 91:1-16; 119:114)

h. You grow in your relationship and assurance of salvation (1 Peter 2:2-3; Eph 4:15; Col 1:10; 1 Jn 5:13)

i. You grow and become equipped for good work (2 Tim 3:14-17; Rom 15:4)

j. You learn to respect the Lord (1 Cor 6:20; Prov 8:23; Deut 17:19-20)

k. Your life will be prosperous, and you will have success (Josh 1:8; Jer 29:11; 1 Kng 2:3; 1 Sam 18:14)

How Do I Deal With Temptation?

Equally important in understanding God's forgiveness is learning how to deal with temptation. God intends us to gain victory when we are tempted. Also, God does not expect us to confess temptation but merely to recognize it as temptation and to say "NO" to it as an act of our will.

I. What is temptation?

   a. Temptation is the work of the devil reaching out to our "natural" sinful self (1 Peter 5:8; Luke 22:3,31; Mark 4:15; 2 Cor 2:11; 1 Chronicles 21:1) who:

     1. Is subtle and offers what only appears to be good (Gen 3:1-13; 2 Cor 11:3,14,15)

     2. Causes us to question God's Word (Gen 3:1)

     3. Causes us to question God's character (Gen 3:4-5)

     4. Lures and entices us with our own desires (Gen 3:6; James 1:13-15) which are: (1 John 2:15-17 and illustrated in Gen 3:6; Isa 14:12-14; Matt 4:1-11; Mark 4:19)

       a) Lust of the flesh – desire to indulge, fulfilling any desire outside of the will of God Satan's effort to get us out of the will of God. (Gal 5:16-17)

       b) Lust of the eyes – the desire for possessions (coveting that which God does not allow at this particular time or place (Matt 6:24-34; 1 Tim 6:9-10) Satan's effort to get us to distrust God.

c) Pride of Life – desire to impress, self-glorification, self-confidence or independence from God (1 Cor 1:26-31; Deut 8:11-18) Satan's effort to destroy our confidence in God. (1 John 2:16)

Remember, lust can be a desire for something wrong or desire to receive something good but in the wrong way.

5. Satan prompts people to tempt us (Matt 18:7; Prov 1:10-19) through

a) Wickedness of evil men (2 Tim 3:12-14; Prov 2:12-15; 16:29)

b) Lack of sensitivity and thoughtfulness of fellow-Christians (Rom 14:13-21; 1 Cor 10:28-32)

c) Wrong teachings of false prophets (Mark 13:21-22; 2 Peter 2:1-20)

d) Seductions of an immoral woman (Prov 2:16; 6:24-29,32-33; and Proverbs chapters 5 and 7)

6. Satan has his ability limited by God (Job 1:10-12; 2:6; Luke 22:31-32; James 4:7; Eph 6:11; 1 Pet 5:8-9)

II. Why we need victory over temptation:

a. Without victory, we surrender to sin and suffer the consequences (Rom 2:6-11; James 1:14-15)

b. Victory over temptation leads us to a victorious walk with God (Isa 33:15-16; Prov 13:14; 14:27; 28:10)

c. Angels come and minister to us amidst victory (Matt 4:11)

d. Jesus prayed for our victory (Luke 22:31-32)

e. Because we have two natures as Christians, and we are commanded to yield to our new nature (Rom 6:12-13; Gal 5:17)

f. Without victory, the labor of others in our lives to help us will be in vain (1 Thess 3:5)

g. Satan has already won too many victories (1 Tim 5:15)

h. Because God has promised us a way of escape and victory in _any_ temptation (1 Cor 10:13; 2 Thess 3:3; 2 Peter 2:9; 1 John 4:4)

III. How to have victory over temptation: (James 4:7-8)

a. Submit to God (example of not submitting: Rom 10:3)

   1. Develop a reverence for God (Matt 22:36-38; Prov 14:27; Ps 73:25-26;)

   2. Be involved in the Word of God   (Ps 119:105; Ps 119:9,11,165; Matt 4:1-11; Job 31:1-40)

Memorize a few select verses on the particular area of temptation and meditate on them in order to know how to deal scripturally with it. Then, in order not to focus on the temptation, memorize and meditate on a few verses of praise to God to focus your attention on Jesus and His character.

3. Set your heart on hating evil (Isa 33:15-16; Ps 97:10; 119:104; Rom 12:9)

4. Ask God to show you His way of escape or endurance and trust Him for it (1 Cor 10:13; Gen 20:6; 2 Peter 2:9; Heb 2:18; 4:15-16)

5. Ask God to show you how to apply the principles of His Word to your specific situation. (Ps 16:11; Ps 25:4; Eze 20:10-12; Mic 6:8)

6. Walk in obedience (Rom 12:21; Deut 8:11-18; Isa 48:17-18; John 14:21-24)

7. As an act of your will, yield to and grow your new nature (Rom 6:12-14; Eph 4:22-24,27; Col 3:10)

8. Be in submission to authority (Heb 13:17; 1 Thess 5:12-13; Jer 35:5-17)

b. Resist the Devil (1 Pet 5:8-10)

1. Recognize the devices of Satan (2 Cor 2:10-11)

2. Flee (1 Cor 6:18 ; 10:14; 1 Tim 6:10-11; 2 Tim 2:22-23; Prov 27:12)

a) Situations you know will tempt you (2 Tim 2:22; Deut 7:25; Matt 18:8-9; Gen 39:7-10)

b) Wrong friendships by giving intimate associations to Godly people (Prov 1:10-17; 4:14-15; 13:20; Ex 34:12; John 15:15; Heb 10:25). We must have associations and friendships with non-believers, but we cannot put ourselves into close intimate relationships with non-believers who can lead us to sin.

c) Listening to and pursuing false doctrines and teachers (Matt 7:15; 2 Peter 3:17; Prov 19:27; Jer 23:16; 1 Jn 4:1-3; Acts 20:29-30)

c. Claim (Rom 6:11)

1. Our position in Christ of victory over the devil that gives him no right to win over us (Col 2:13-15; Heb 2:14-18; 1 John 4:4)

2. By watching and praying for victory (Col 4:2; 1 Cor 16:13; Ps 60:12; 119:133; Jude 24; Luke 11:4)

Do not confess temptation. A momentary glance at something that comes into view or a thought that pops into your head is not sin until you concentrate on it or act on it. Confessing temptation often causes us to go ahead and sin under the pretense of confession. Satan traps us by having us say, "Lord, forgive me for almost...." By naming in detail what the sin WOULD have been, we actually do then commit it (Matt 5:27-28). Temptation doesn't become sin until we willfully say "yes" to dwelling (focusing) upon or acting upon the wrong thought, attitude or action.

Trials

Every circumstance we face can be both a trial and a temptation. Not only do bad circumstances and thoughts constitute a trial (God wants to teach us to rejoice and walk by faith), but good circumstances and thoughts are also a trial because God wants us to glorify Him and depend more on Him because of those good things (Ex 16:4; Ps 116:1-2). Likewise, good circumstances and thoughts are a temptation just as bad circumstances and thoughts are. Here Satan not only wants us to be bitter over the "bad" things but also to become independent (looking to ourselves rather than to God) because of the "good" things that happen in our lives.

Once we learn to see each thought and circumstance as both a trial and a temptation (depending upon how we react), learn how to deal with each, and discipline ourselves to obedience by the power of the Holy Spirit who resides within each Christian, victory in the Christian life can become a reality.

I.   What is a trial?

   a. The work of God (Gen 22:1; Ps 66:10-12; Zech 13:9; Job 23:10; Ps 139:23-24) who:

   b. Tests the mind and heart (Ps 26:2-3; 1 Chron 29:17) by humbling us (Deut 8:2) in order to:

      1.   Know what is in your heart (Deut 8:2; 2 Chron 32:30,31)

      2.   See if you will obey (Deut 8:2; Judges 2:21,22)

3. Make God's Word be your very life (Deut 8:3; John 6:63; Ps 119:71-72)
4. Let you know that God is sufficient to meet every need (Deut 8:4; Philippians 4:19)
5. Discipline you (Deut 8:5) Discipline means training up as a child and includes both Godly habits and chastisement for wrongdoing.

c. Tests our faith (James 1:2-3) by allowing circumstances to lead us to have to be decisive and to develop a value system (James 1:5-11) in order to:

1. Produces steadfastness (James 1:3)
2. Produces spiritual maturity (James 1:4)
3. Produces satisfaction with God's provision (James 1:4)
4. Teaches you to ask in faith for wisdom to handle circumstances (James 1:5-6)
5. Produces stability (James 1:7-8)
6. Produces an eternal value system (James 1:9-11)

d. Allows us to share in Christ's sufferings (1 Peter 4:12-13; Phil 3:10) in order to produce:

1. Endurance \ Perseverance (Rom 5:3-5) which produces
2. Character (Rom 5:3-5) which produces
3. Hope (Rom 5:3-5)
4. Comfort (2 Cor 1:3-6)
5. Testimony to comfort others (2 Cor 1:4-6)

6. Trust in the sufficiency of God's grace (2 Cor 1:8-9; 2 Cor 12:9)
7. To be proved as an heir and glorified with Him (Rom 8:17)
8. Teach obedience (Heb 5:7-10)

e. Tests our love for Him by allowing false prophets to predict events accurately and then they suggest following other gods (Deut 13:1-5)

II. Why we face trial:

a. Trials are evidence of God's righteous judgment (2 Thess 1:4-5)
b. Enduring trial leads to the crown of life (James 1:12)
c. Trials develop a genuine faith which yields praise, glory, and honor to Jesus Christ (1 Peter 1:6-7)
d. Enduring insults for the name of Christ brings the Spirit of God's glory to rest upon us (1 Peter 4:14)
e. Trials refine us and bless us (Ps 66:10-12; Dan 12:10)
f. Trials allow the works of God to show through our lives (John 9:2-3; 2 Cor 4:11)
g. Trials are to shine forth the glory of God (John 11:4; 2 Cor 4:17-18)
h. Trials are a pruning tool to enable us to bear more fruit (John 15:2; Phil 1:12-14)

III. How to have victory in a trial:

a. Rejoice (James 1:2; 1 Peter 4:12-13)

1. Realize your secure position in Christ (Rom 8:35-39)

2. Realize God allowed the trial and ask Him what He is doing in your life (Job 23:10; Ps 94:12-13).

3. Recognize that God's answer to what He is doing maybe that He is teaching you to trust and rely upon Him, even when you do not understand (Isa 50:10)

4. Actively thank God for the situation and for what He is doing in your life (1 Thess 5:16-18; Eph 5:20)

b. Ask in faith for wisdom on how to deal with the trial (James 1:5-6; 1 Kings 3:9; Prov 2:1-9)

c. Endure (James 1:12; 2 Thess 1:3-5; Heb 6:13-15; 11:27)

1. Continue rejoicing
2. Continue to obey the wisdom God gives

TRIAL CHART

Kind	Identifications	Result
Trial of the Heart and Mind. Ps 26:2-3	We are put in a situation where we are humbled. Deut 8:1-2	God wants to produce: obedience (Jn 14:21) a heart for God's Word (Deut 8:3) God is our provider (Deut 8:4) a disciplined life (Deut 8:5)
Trial of our Faith. James 1:2-4	We are in a situation where we must be decisive, where we must develop an eternal value system to make the correct decisions. 1 Sam 24	God wants to produce: Steadfastness (James 1:3), He makes us perfect, complete and we lack nothing (Phil 4:11-13), He promises wisdom, decisiveness, an eternal value system and a Crown of Life. (2 Tim 1:7; James 1:12)
Trial of Suffering. Rom 5:3-5	When you hurt physically and/or emotionally.	God wants to produce: endurance, character, hope (Rom 5:3-5), He wants to comfort others through us (2 Cor 1:4), He wants us to develop an attitude of prayer (2 Cor 1:10-11)
Trial of Love. Deut 13:1-4	When we are in a situation where someone offers us an attractive answer to a felt need but it will require us to follow other gods. Gen 3:1-13	He wants to produce: obedience, service to God, close intimate fellowship with Him (Deut 13:4)

Meditation

The most important element of transforming and refocusing our thoughts is meditating on the Lord and His Word.

I. What is meditation? (Josh 1:8):

   a. Continual delighting in God's Word (Ps 1:1-3; 119:15,16,23,48,59,78,97-99,148; Deut 6:6-7)
   b. A function of the heart (Ps 4:4; 19:14) Set your affections on God and His Word and works.
   c. Thinking about God's works (Ps 77:12; 143:5; Col 3:1-2)
   d. Thinking about who God is (Rev 1:8; Ps 77:10-12; 119:55-56)
   e. Thinking about how my life lines up with the ways of God (Ps 119:57-64; Rom 7:15-20)

II. Why do we need to meditate?

   a. It is commanded (Josh 1:8)
   b. It brings satisfaction and praise (Ps 63:5-6)
   c. It brings joy (Ps 104:34)
   d. It makes me wiser than my enemies (Ps 119:98)
   e. It gives more understanding than my teachers (Ps 119:99; 49:3)
   f. Because God's thoughts are precious to us (Ps 139:17-18)
   g. It is necessary for obedience which produces prosperity and success (Josh 1:8; 1 Kings 2:1-3)

h. Leads us to turn from sin (Ps 119:9-11)
i. It brings insight into correct responses in persecution – seeing persecution from God's point of view (Ps 119:23,78)
j. Because what controls our mind controls us, God commands us to meditate in order to help us (Rom 8;5-9; Pr 27:19) in order to give us:

   1. A transformed life (Rom 12:2)
   2. A selfless life (Phil 2:3-8)
   3. A Spirit-controlled life (Col 3:2-3)
   4. A peaceful life (Isa 26:3)

III. How to meditate:

a. Memorize the Word (Deut 11:18-19). When you memorize a verse or passage be sure to quote the book, chapter, and verse both before and after the verse. You must remember where the verse came from to share it effectively with others.

b. Expand your understanding of passages of the Word

   1. Ask questions about the verses
   2. Emphasize different words in the verses and think on what they mean with that particular emphasis (YOUR Word is a light... Your WORD is a light... Your Word IS a light...)
   3. In your own life and that of others, how has God worked to fulfill these verses?

4. What does God want you to do as a result of what He has taught you from these verses today?

c. Personalize the verses – put personal pronouns and your name, when possible into the verses

d. Visualize the verse – develop a mental picture of what the verses mean and of yourself doing what God wants you to do. Draw a diagram or picture.

e. Harmonize the verses (Col 3:16) sing the verses back to God.

Meditation is spiritual digestion; it is getting the Word of God from the head to the heart and in the life. God wants us to react unconsciously with righteousness not just act out from our old sin nature.

Gaining a Clear Conscience

To understand God's forgiveness of sin and our need to confess sin that He has revealed in our life, it is essential for us to see the importance of maintaining a clear conscience.

I. What is a clear conscience?

    a. Living without offense toward God and toward man (Acts 24:16; 1 Cor 10:32)

    b. Living without self-condemnation (1 John 3:20,21; Rom 2:12-16; 2 Cor 1:12)

    c. Walking in the light – being totally transparent with each other, especially in feelings and attitudes (1 John 1:5-7; 2 Cor 4:2)

II. Why we need a clear conscience:

    a. So that your life backs up your verbal ministry (1 Peter 3:16; 2 Cor 4:1,2)

    b. Not having a clear conscience leads to a lack of boldness in witnessing (1 Peter 3:16; Prov 28:1)

    c. Your lack of a clear conscience may cause weaker brothers and sisters around you to stumble (Rom 14:21; 1 Cor 8:7-13; Matt 18:7)

    d. A clear conscience is part of the obedient Christian life (1 Tim 1:5; Heb 10:22)

    e. Without a clear conscience, our faith may be shipwrecked (1 Tim 1:19; Matt 27:3-5)

f. Lack of a clear conscience may cause us to imagine things that are not true (Mark 6:14-16)

g. Health and physical appearance depend on a clear conscience (Ps 32:1,3,4; Gen 4:5-7)

h. Lack of a clear conscience may lead God to give you up to worse things in order to bring you to repentance (Rom 1:18-32)

i. Without a clear conscience, you cannot love people (1 Tim 1:5; 1 John 4:20,21)

III. How to obtain a clear conscience:

a. Toward God

1. Study, understand and apply the how to's of "Receiving God's Forgiveness" study (1 Peter 3:21; 1 John 1:9)

2. To maintain a clear conscience toward God, be willing even to bear up under unjust suffering and sorrow (1 Peter 2:19; see study on "Trials")

b. Toward People

1. List their offenses against you personally (not against others). It is important to not take up offenses made against others and create a root of bitterness in our own personal lives (Heb 12:15).

2. List your offenses to others that you have been made aware of. Sometimes there is a progressive revelation of offenses, meaning as we deal with

one set or level another set or level becomes apparent (Ps 32:5).

3. Purpose to gain forgiveness of the ones you have offended (Matt 5:23,24)

i. Privately relive your offenses from their point of view, their feelings. This can produce a genuine sorrow for what you have done (James 4:8-10).

ii. Act quickly to ask forgiveness (Matt 5:23-24)

   a. Identify the basic offense. It is useless to ask forgiveness without getting to your real attitude and/or action that offended them.

   b. Work out the proper wording in detail

      i. Do not project blame by saying "If I was wrong…"

      ii. Do not use the word "sorry," because it does not communicate genuineness and repentance.

      iii. Be sure to include:

         1. "God has convicted me about my …. "
         2. "I was wrong"
         3. "Will you please forgive me"
         4. Wait for them to respond in silence

5. Ask for forgiveness in person maybe by phone, but never in writing, e-mail, text
6. Avoid sharing shameful details, stick to the basic offense (Eph 5:12)

iv. Make restitution when needed (Luke 19:8-9)

v. If at this point you are not forgiven, it may be because:

1. You have upset their guilt-blame balance (If they forgive you, they no longer can blame you and would have only guilt left)

2. They may want to see a change in your behavior (Luke 3:8)

3. You may have failed to hit the basic offense

4. Fully forgive their offenses toward you in your own heart (Matt 6:14-15; 18:15,21,22). Do not take on a "Holier-than-thou" attitude (an attitude of moral superiority) and pronounce your forgiveness of their offenses toward you. Do it in your heart and show them the change of heart through love actions and a changed attitude.

a. View offender as a tool of God (Gen 50:20)

b. Recognize offense as God's working in you to: (1 Thess 5:18; 2 Sam 16:5-13)

i. To reveal wrong attitudes in you which must be dealt with

ii. To reveal the needs of the offender which you can pray for and be available to meet (Acts 16:16-18; Luke 6:27-30). Be willing to suffer if necessary, to heal the offender (Luke 23:34)

c. React to the offender through love and good deeds, instead of bitterness and revenge (Rom 12:19-20). Remember, that offender may be God's messenger to you for growing more maturity in Christ within you and for you to receive a blessing.

It is possible that the other person was not offended or professes not to have been offended. Leave it with simply noting your concern that you had caused an offense and that you will work on that issue in your own life so that it will not come up again with them or others.

Remember, confession is not a time to discuss other issues. It is not to be used as an opportunity for witnessing. The confession should be no broader than your offense and must not be so graphic as to dredge up all the awful parts of what happened in the other person's mind.

How to Have a Good Self-Image

I. What is self-acceptance?

a. Realizing you are created in God's image (Gen 1:26-27; 5:1-2). You are a triune (three-part) being (mind, will, emotion) just as God is triune (Father, Son, Holy Spirit).

b. Realizing God created you to fulfill His unique purposes for you (Ps 139:13-16; Job 31:15; 33:4; Ps 100:3; 119:73) such as:

   1. To love God (Matt 22:36-38; Hos 6:3,6)
   2. To fellowship with God (1 Cor 1:9; Phil 3:10)
   3. To do good works (Eph 2:10; Titus 2:13-14; Matt 5:16)
   4. To proclaim the excellences of Christ to others (1 Peter 2:9)
   5. To bring glory to God (1 Cor 10:31; Isa 43:7; 63:11-14)

c. Realizing that the redeemed man is the glory of God (2 Cor 3:18; Rom 8:28-30; 1 Cor 11:7)

d. A good self-image is a function of the soul (mind, will and emotions) (Ps 139:14) and so must be built by believing God on the battlefield of the mind (Rom 12:2; Isa 26:3; Col 3:2; Prov 27:19)

e. Having a proper view of yourself, (Rom 12:3) you are:

   1. Of no spiritual worth apart from Jesus Christ (John 15:5)
   2. Wretched apart from His righteousness (Rom 7:22-25)

3. You possess all of the character and power of Jesus Christ when you claim it (James 1:5; Matt 18:18; 2 Tim 1:7; Phil 4:13; Eph 2:1-10)

II. How to develop a good self-image:

    a. Confess all areas of self-rejection and ungratefulness (1 Jn 1:9; Prov 28:13)

    b. Thank God for the things you cannot change such as your appearance, abilities, parentage and social environment (Ps 139:14; 1 Thess 5:18; Eph 5:20). View unchangeable factors in these areas as signs of God's ownership of you (1 Cor 6:19-20)

    c. Commit yourself to allow God to continue to develop the character of Christ in you (Gal 4:19; Eph 4:11-13)

    d. Commit yourself to allow God to reproduce the character of Christ through you into the lives of others (Matt 28: 16-20; Phil 1:21-26; 2 Cor 1:3-6; 2 Cor 3:2).

Stop comparing yourself to others. God is interested in you and what He has invested in you through everything that has been in your life up until this moment. Those blessings and even the pain have made you who you are and that cannot be compared to anything He has done in the lives of others around you. It is good to strive to be better and more than you are now, but it is harmful (sin) to compare your life to others and covet what they have.

God's Vision For The World

I. What is God's vision for the world?

   a. To seek and to save the lost (Luke 5:32; Luke 19:10)

   b. To bring the saved to spiritual maturity (Col 1:28-29)

   c. To use men and women to accomplish these objectives (Matt 4:19; John 17:18; John 20:21; 2 Cor 2:14-17; 2 Tim 2:2; 3 John 4; Phil 1:21-26)

II. Why do we need God's vision?

   a. Where there is no vision the people perish (Prov 29;18)

   b. God commanded us to have His vision (Matt 28:18-20; John 17:18; 20:21)

   c. Having God's vision glorifies Him (2 Thess 1:11-12)

   d. The Gospel has been entrusted to us (1 Thess 2:4)

   e. We are to give our lives to that which is eternal (Matt 6:19-21)

   f. It brings us the greatest possible joy (3 John 4; Phil 4:1; 1 Thess 2:19,20)

   g. Without it, we cannot fulfill God's purpose for our lives (Matt 5:16; John 15:8)

III. How to develop and fulfill God's vision:

   a. Evangelize (witness), tell others what God has done in your life and what He can do in theirs as well (1 Cor 9:16-17; 2 Cor 5:16-20; 1 Thess 1:4-2:16; 2 Tim 1:7-8; 4:2; 4:5)

   b. Make disciples (2 Tim 2:1-2; Josh 11:15; 1 Cor 4:6; Ps 78:70-72)

      1. Become involved in the lives of many people (Matt 13:1-9, 18-23; 2 Tim 4:2)

2. Concentrate on a few people who show a hunger for God (2 Tim 2:2; Mark 3:13-18)
3. Lead by example (1 Cor 4:6; 4:14-17; 11:1; Phil 3:17; 1 Thess 1:5-8; 2 Tim 3:10-11; Heb 13:7-8,17)
4. Show them how to transform their minds with the Word of God (Rom 12:2; 8:5-8; Phil 2:5-8 Ps 119:11; 24:3-4; 51:10; Prov 3:1-6)
5. Give them a vision for the lost (Mark 6:30-44; Luke 10:1-21)
6. Prayerfully give them unforgettable instructions (1 Sam 12:23-24; 1 Thess 1:2-4)
7. Build up their faith, love and hope (2 Thess 1:3-4; Heb 11:1,6; John 13:34-35; Rom 8:24-25)

Much of our growth as Christians comes from following the example of others. None of us are perfect, but we need to follow the example of those who are more mature in their faith than we are. In Philippians 3:17-21 Paul encouraged them to follow the example which he, Timothy and Epaphroditus had set before them and not follow those who teach a different gospel. Is your life a model for someone else to follow? Would you want someone to follow in your footsteps? No matter who you are, someone is watching your life. Make the changes necessary and start leading on a path to Christlikeness.

The Lordship of Christ

I.   What is the Lordship of Jesus Christ?

   a.   Giving Christ His rightful place in my life
        (John 13:13; Phil 2:9-11; Luke 6:46-49)
   b.   The total commitment of every area of my life to Him
        (Phil 3:7-14; Luke 14:26-27; 14:33)
   c.   Absolute obedience (Luke 6:46; Ex 7:6; 2 Kings 5:13-
        14; Jn 14:15)
   d.   A deep attitude of heart, not merely outward actions
        (Gal 2:20)

        1.   Christ is the only necessary thing in my life –
             everything else is trash by comparison
             (Phil 3:7-8)

        2.   Pride is dead (Phil 3:9)

             i.   Realize that in my sin nature there is no good
                   thing (Jer 17:9; Ps 16:2; Rom 7:18).

             ii.   Realize Jesus alone is my sufficiency (2 Cor 3:5;
                   12:19; Col 2:10; Heb 10:14)

             iii. My deepest heart desire is to know God
                   intimately and be influenced by Him
                   (Phil 3:10)

    iv.   Willingness to experience His resurrection life daily (Phil 3:10b) by believing it, speaking it and living it.

    v.   Willingness to die to self and endure suffering (Phil 3:10c; 1:29; Gal 2:20; 2 Tim 2:8-13)

II. Why we need to make Christ Lord of our lives:

  a. Jesus desires it (2 Cor 5:15)

  b. Jesus deserves it because of

     1. Who He is (Phil 2:9-11)
     2. What He did (Rom 14:9)
     3. What He wants to do (John 10:10; Col 2:9-15; 1 Jn 3:9-10)

  c. His Lordship is the only power source for the abundant Christian life (John 15:5)

  d. He is the only one capable of meeting the deepest needs and longings of my heart (John 6:67-69; Col 2:9-10)

  e. Knowing Jesus as Load is worth more than anything else (Phil 3:7-8; Luke 14:33; Heb 11:24-26)

  f. Abiding in (Obeying) Him is the only way we can bear fruit (John 15:1-6; 1 John 2:6; 3:24)

III. How to make and keep Christ as Lord:

  a. By decision (Rom 12:1; Ps 73:25-26; 1 Peter 3:15a)
  b. Daily (Luke 9:23)

  i. The practical outworking of the Lordship of Christ in my life is the Holy Spirit who enters believers at conversion is at work in and through me as I keep sin confessed and I surrender daily to do the will of Christ in my life (Eph 5:17-18)

ii. Some outward evidences of Christ as Lord of my life (the Holy Spirit at work in me) are:

1. Encouraging others from God's Word (Eph 5:19; Heb 3:13; 10:25; 1 Thess 5:11)
2. A joyful heart that delights in His presence (Eph 5:19; Ps 27:4; Phil 4:4)
3. Giving thanks in all circumstances (Eph 5:20; 1 Thess 5:18; James 1:2-3; see study on "Trials")
4. Submitting to others (deferring to other's needs) (Eph 5:21; Phil 2:3-4)
5. Godly family relationships (Eph 5:21-6:4)
6. Godly working relationships (Eph 6:5-9; Col 3:22-24)

   a. Employees – submit and work heartily unto the Lord and not until men (your boss is not the one in the office, it is God Himself and what you do at your job and how you approach work should show that know you are responsible to God first).

   b. Employers – encourage employees and do not use threats in order to motivate them.

7. Involvement in the warfare of prayer (Eph 6:10-20)
8. Godly character (Gal 5:22-25; Jer 17:10; Acts 13:22; 17:11; Rom 12:17; Eph 5:1-2).

Prayer

"Rejoice in the Lord always; again I will say, rejoice! Let your gentle spirit be known to all men, The Lord is near. Be anxious for nothing, but in everything by prayer and supplication with thanksgiving let your requests be made known to God. And the peace of God, which surpasses all comprehension, will guard your hearts and minds in Christ Jesus." (Ryrie Study Bible NAS Philippians 4:4-7)

Paul makes it clear in Romans 8:26-27 and Eph 6:18 that the only kind of effective praying is what he calls praying in the Holy Spirit.

I.   What is praying in the Holy Spirit? It is exemplified in the Lord's Prayer Luke 11:1-4 and John chapter 17.

   a.   Talking to God (1 Tim 2:1; Ps 5:3; Jer 33:3)

   1. Adoration, acknowledge who He is in our life

      i.   Adore Him – tell God how great He is
            (1 Chron 29:10-13; 1 Tim 1:17)
      ii.   Worship Him – recognize who He is
            (Ps 100:1-4; 103:1-4; Isa 40:1-31, Ps 136,)
      iii. Praise Him – tell God how great He is doing
            (Isa 12:5-6; Ps 70:4; Ps 148 through 150)

   2. Confession (Ps 24:3-6; Ps 32:5; James 5:16; 1 Jn 1:9-10)

   3. Thanksgiving (1 Thess 5:18; Col 4:2, Rev 7:11-12;
       Ps 100:4-5)

4. Offering supplications to Him for my own and other's needs and desires (Phil 4:6-7; James 5:13-18)

5. Interceding to Him for others' needs (1 Sam 12:23; Ex 32:11-14) – standing between the judgment of God and someone else in order to see God change the course of their life (Luke 22:31-32; Matt 5:44)

II. Why do we need to pray in the Spirit?

    a. It is commanded (Col 4:2)
    b. God desires it (Ex 29:45; Lev 26:12; Ps 27:8; 1 Jn 1:3)
    c. God's work is limited without it (James 4:2b-3)
    d. Jesus set the example (Mark 1:35; Luke 6:12)
    e. To receive God's blessings (Matt 7:7-11)
    f. Our joy is incomplete without it (John 16:24)
    g. For healing (James 5:16; 2 Chron 7:14)
    h. To gain wisdom (James 1:5)
    i. Because of our priesthood (1 Peter 2:5)
    j. It is the key to victorious living (Ps 50:15; 55:22)
    k. Satan has no defense against it (Luke 22:31-32; Eph 6:10-18)
    l. For mercy and help in the time of need (Heb 4:16)
    m. God is looking for pray-ers (Ezek 22:30; Ps 106:23)
    n. It brings peace and awareness of Christ (Phil 4:6-7)

III. How to pray in the Spirit:

    a. Meet the prerequisites to pray successfully –

        1. Be still and wait longingly for Him (Ps 46:10; 62:5)
        2. Have all known sin confessed (Isa 59:1-2; Ps 66:18 2 Chron 16:9a)

3. Commit yourself to an abiding relationship with Jesus Christ (John 15:7)

    i. Acknowledge your only purpose in life is to bear fruit (John 15:4-6; Isa 43:4; Gal 5:22-23)

    ii. Commit yourself to bear any kind of fruit God wants to produce through you (John 15:8)

    iii. Commit yourself to trust God and obey Him even before He tells you what to do (2 Sam 7:28; Ps 9:10; Prov 3:5-6; John 15:9-11)

4. Bind Satan from hindering or confusing your mind while you pray (Eph 6:11-12; Heb 2:14-18; Matt 16:19; 18:18)

5. Acknowledge your inability to pray, ask the Holy Spirit to show you what to pray (Rom 8:26-27)

b. Pour your heart out to God (Ps 62:8)

1. Be bold (Luke 11:5-13; Heb 4:16)
2. Be persistent (Luke 11:8; 18:1-8)

    i. Be confident God will answer (1 John 5:14-15; Matt 21:22)

    God answers three ways – yes, no and wait

    ii. We are to pray constantly (1 Thess 5:16-18; Eph 6:18)

"This is the confidence which we have before Him, that, if we ask anything according to His will, He hears us. And if we know that He hears us in whatever we ask, we know that we have the requests which we have asked from Him." 1 John 5:14-15 Ryrie Study Bible NAS

Prayer: communicating to God that which He has laid upon my heart to speak

Keep a prayer diary with the petitions asked, dates asked, and dates received. See sample Journal on page 7 above.

Importance of God's Word

The Bible is the complete Word of God given to mankind for guidance into heaven and for education in Christianity to be lived out here on this earthly existence.

Peter writes in 2 Peter 1:20,21: *"But I know this first of all, that no prophecy of Scripture is a matter of one's own interpretation, for no prophecy was ever made by an act of human will, but men moved by the Holy Spirit spoke from God."* Peter then goes on in chapter two to warn of false teachers. Proverbs 30:5,6 states *"Every word of God is tested; He is a shield to those who take refuge in Him. Do not add to His words or He will reprove you, and you will be proved a liar."* John in the final part of Revelation in 22:18 states, *"I testify to everyone who hears the words of the prophecy of this book: if anyone adds to them, God will add to him the plagues which are written in this book: and if anyone takes away from the words of the book of this prophecy, God will take away his part from the tree of life and from the holy city, which is written in this book."* The apostle Paul was very specific about anyone trying to add to or adulterate the Gospel of Jesus Christ. In Galatians 1:6-9 he writes, *"I am amazed that you are so quickly deserting Him who called you by the grace of Christ, for a different gospel; which is really not another; only there are some who are disturbing you and want to distort the gospel of Christ. But even if we, or an angel from heaven, should preach to you a gospel contrary to what we have preached to you, he is to be accursed! As we have said before so I say again, now, if any*

*man is preaching to you a gospel contrary to what you received,
he is to be accursed!"* (all quotes *Ryrie Study Bible NAS*)

I.   Christian's Life Goal can be summarized as follows:

*"To know, love and glorify God and to be used of
Him to raise up qualified laborers in significant
numbers, as fast as is possible to help fulfill the
Great Commission."*

   a.   To know God: Why should we KNOW God?

      1. It is His desire. When Adam and Eve sinned, God
sought them out. He continues to seek men and
women today. It is His desire to fellowship with
us. (Rom 5:8; 1 Jn 1:3; 1 Cor 1:9; Job 7:17-18)

      2. It should be our desire as well. (Phil 3:10;
Ps 27:4; Ex 33:11 (note where Joshua stayed),13;
Gen 24:63)

      3. The results of knowing God. To know Him is to
become like Him and to please Him (Ps 1:1-3;
John 17:3; 1 Thess 2:12; 2 Cor 5:9;)

      4. How do we get to know God?

         i.   Through His Word the Bible
         ii. By spending time with Him in study and
prayer

   b.   To Love God, We hear a lot about the Great
Commission (Mark 16:15-18) but perhaps not nearly

enough about the Great Commandment
(Matt 22:34-40)

1. Loving God is a matter of choice (Deut 30:19-20)
   Loving God begins with an act of the will. Our
   emotions are subject to our will not our will to our
   emotions. Therefore, loving God is basically an act of
   the will.

2. Love for God is the basis for obedience. (Deut 5:29;
   1 John 5:2-5) To love God is to trust Him and to trust
   Him is to obey Him. Whenever we disobey God, we
   are saying two things:

   i.   "God, you do not have my best interest at heart."
        OR

   ii. "God, you do not know what is best for me."
        (Jer 29:11; Heb 11:6)

   THE source for finding out what God wants us to do
   and what He has in store for us is His Word
   (2 Tim 3:16-17).

3. How do we love God? (1 John 2:5; Prov 23:26; Ps
   91:14; 2 John 6; 1 John 5:2-5) If you have someone very
   special in your life, what do the two of you do? You
   spend time together. It is the same with God. You do
   not seek him for what He can give you but just because
   of who He is ... God.

   i.   Ways to love God: increase an intimate
        knowledge of Him through reading the Bible.

ii. Pursue getting to know Him. Ask Him for an unquenchable thirst for Him and His Word (Hosea 6:3)

iii. Spend time searching Him out and being with Him in His Word and in prayer (Eph 5:15-16; John 14:15,21)

iv. We love God because we are overwhelmed by His love for us. (I John 4:19)

c. To Glorify God

1. The purpose for which we were created is to Glorify God (Isa 43:7; Rev 4:11; 1 Cor 6:19-20)

2. Glorifying God is commanded (1 Cor 10:31, Col 3:23)

3. Glorifying God is explained (John 15:8; Eph 6:7)

[1]Know God
Phil 3:10

[6]Glorify God
1 Cor 10:31

[2]Love God
Mt 22:36-38

[5]Please God
John 14:21

[3]Trust God
Prov 3:5-6

[4]Obey God
John 15:10

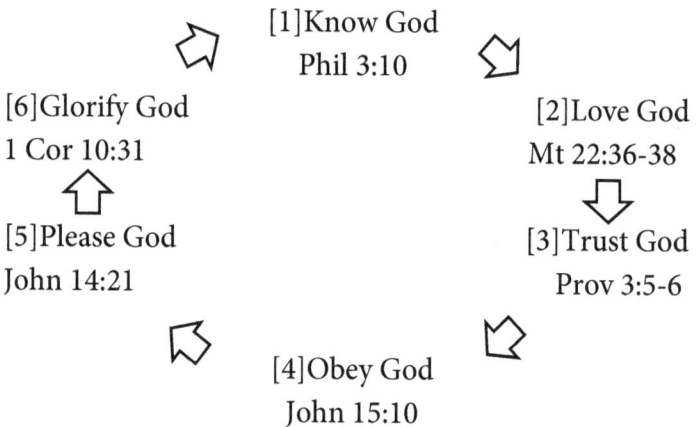

Notice the sequence: Know-Love-Glorify. How can we glorify God if we don't first know and love Him? Both love and knowledge come from spending daily time with Him in this Word and in prayer.

II. There are therefore some unchangeable spiritual laws about knowing God

   a. Matt 4:4; Deut 8:3 states that we cannot live without the Word of God.

   b. 2 Tim 3:16-17 states that the Word has a distinct purpose and it has unquestionable validity.

      1. The Word is our only tangible connection with God. We were not physically at the cross, but He has told us about this and much more.

      2. The Word is profitable for several things:

         i. Teaching: to show us God's way Ps 25:4

         ii. Reproof: to keep us from straying from God's way

         iii. Correction: to bring us back on to the way of God if and when we do stray.

         iv. Training: to show us how to stay on God's way, also food to make us strong.

   c. Job 23:12 states what our purpose should be. If we do not meet with God daily for spiritual food and fellowship, we really rebuke God because He always prepares food for us for our daily meetings. We will live in defeat every day we do not meet with Him so that He may prepare us for the day and give us victorious vital food.

III. Five plus ways of consuming God's Word

    a. Hearing: Preaching, Broadcasts, etc. We must learn to take knowledgeable notes to retain information given to us (Rev 1:3: Deut 17:9-20)

    b. Reading: This cleanses our minds. In other words: put in the good stuff and force out the bad stuff in our minds and hearts(John 7:38; James 1:21; Heb 4:12: Ps 119:105; Isa 40:8).

    c. Study: This is where you get into the real depth of the Word. You take it apart, look at it, then put it back together again and look at it some more. This can be done individually but best in a Bible study group with a mature leader (Ezra 7:10)

    d. Memorize the Word: This is an essential step to victory in the Christian life as God promised (Josh 1:8; Ps 119:15; Ps 119:97-98). It is also essential in order to meditate on God's Word.

    e. Saturation: Fill up your storehouse of knowledge then as you go through each day and use what God has taught you. Knowledge unused is knowledge unlearned (Deut 32:46-47).

IV. Sharing: Everything that you learn in the process of growing in the knowledge of God is important for your own spiritual life. Putting that knowledge into everyday practice in your own life is of the first importance but sharing what God has shown you with others must be part of your day to day experience. The more you share, the more that knowledge becomes a part of your own life. Just like the Manna God gave the Israelites during the journey from Egypt to the promised land, if you keep something God has provided to you only in your own mind and life (hoarding it) it will mold and spoil (Ex 16:19-20).

V. Types of Bible studies. Try different study methods to bring out the depth of understanding available to you from the Bible:

a. Sequences:

1. Look for sequences in scripture. The way things are listed and/or their sequence in scripture is important. For example, the beatitudes in Matt 5:1-11 or Church life in Acts 2:42.

2. Look for conclusions, cause and effect sequences, understanding why something happened and what outcome or affect it had and its importance such as Matt 9:20-22

b. Character Studies. These are always good to trace a person's life through scripture and see how he reacted to God and this world, for example, David or Paul.

c. Topical Studies: Every topic imaginable is spoken of somewhere or alluded to in the Bible. This type of study can reinforce your walk with God on specific ideas or questions. The topical references in the companion book in this series (Christianity, Bible References by Topic) are not complete but have a wealth of references for the topics noted.

Practical Pointers from "A Plan for Spiritual Growth and Health" by Peter M. Lord:

Time: Have your time alone with God at the same time every day. It will be hard to start this habit but having it at the same time every day will be easier.

Place: Use the same place every day. This will help you establish the habit. A quiet place where there is no noise and you will not be disturbed is best.

Priority: Give this time with God Priority. Do not let other things fill and clutter your mind and heart before or during seeking God.

Persistency: The real value of this program will come as a result of day by day consistency. The hardest time will be on weekends and holidays. Do not allow yourself to go without it – let it be like brushing your teeth – a regular day by day habit.

Witnessing

I. What is witnessing?

    a. Explaining in a clear way what God has done in Jesus Christ, as His ambassador. (2 Cor 5:18-21; 1 Cor 15:3-4)

    b. Exercising the benefits of prayer warfare (Eph 6:10-12; 2 Cor 10:3-5; Matt 18:18)

II. Why witness?

    a. It is commanded of every believer. Not to witness is to be out of the will of God (Luke 19:39-40; 1 Cor 9:16-17; Acts 1:8; Jude 22,23)

    b. Every Christian will be held accountable for his faithfulness to witness (Ezek 3:18-19)

    c. It is God's chosen way to communicate the gospel (Rom 10:14-15; Acts 10:1-6)

    d. People are lost and going to hell forever separated from God and the hope of salvation (Rom 6:23; Matt 25:41; 2 Thess 1:7b-10; John 3:36)

    e. The rewards are great (Acts 20:24; 1 Thess 2:19,20)

    f. We owe it to the lost (Rom 1:14-15)

g. Jesus and the disciples set the example (John 4:7-26; Luke 9:2; Acts 4:18-20; 5:41-42; 17:6)

III. How to Witness:

   a. Prerequisites for an effective witness:

       i.   Know Jesus Christ personally (Acts 4:20; 1 John 1:3)

       ii. Have no unconfessed sin (2 Chron 16:9a; Ps 66:18)

       iii. Be filled with the Holy Spirit (1 Cor 4:20; Zech 4:6)

       iv. Be prepared (1 Peter 3:15; Jer 20:9)

           1. With a method to clearly and simply present the gospel (Rom 1:16)

           2. Be able to share your own testimony of coming to faith in Christ (Rev 12:11; Acts 22, Acts 26)

       v.   Pray, expecting results (Eph 6:18-20; Gal 6:9; Isa 55:11; Rom 10:1)

   b. Having a successful witness:

       i. Make non-Christian contacts (John 4:7-8)

           1. Don't wait for circumstances to be perfect in order to share (Eccl 11:4)

2. Discuss a common interest, then casually turn the conversation to Jesus Christ (John 4:7-8)

ii. Talk about Jesus (John 4:10; 1 Cor 2:1-5)

1. Boldly (Acts 4:13; Eph 6:18-20)

   a. Realize you have all the authority of Jesus in you (Matt 28:18-20; Acts 1:8)

   b. Don't get sidetracked with arguments or questions that aren't really going to change an attitude even if answered (John 4:20; Titus 3:9)

2. Compassionately (Ps 126:5,6; Matt 23:37; 2 Peter 3:9)

3 With gentleness and reverence (1 Peter 3:15)

   a. Don't be pushy – take a person only as far as he is willing to go (John 4:16-26). It has been estimated that it takes about 7-8 times of hearing the Gospel before most people respond. You may be #1 or #8.

   b. Don't condemn, but point out our sin nature and that everyone is separated from God until they accept what Jesus has done for us (Rom 3:23)

4. Use the Word – don't argue about it or defend it. Let it stand on its own. They need to read the passages

themselves aloud, ask what the verse(s) said to them, if they don't understand the verse(s) ask them to read it again. (Heb 4;12; Eph 6:17; 2 Tim 2:24-26)

a. Sow, Cultivate, Reap. These are the three parts to everyone's conversation. There may be multiple people involved with the person through interaction and prayer in this process. You may be a part of one step or part of all in seeing a person accept Christ as their personal savior.

   i. Sow: explain the gospel in a clear way for the first time.

   ii. Cultivate: put new thoughts into another's mind through the Word of God

   iii. Harvest: pick up people when they are ready to receive Jesus Christ.

    1. If you are in regular or occasional contact with a person you can identify with Jesus Christ and what He has done in your own life and share the gospel over time and in part or in full.

    2. If you have only a one-time contact, then it is necessary to simply share the gospel in full.

    3. It is important to be their servant and meet their needs as you come aware of any. It can also mean that you allow them to meet a need you have yourself. (2 Cor 4:5; John 4:7)

Sharing the gospel clearly and in an organized but limited time frame must be practiced. You can start by writing down your own testimony about how you came to Christ. Take out everything that is not completely necessary and get down to about a 2-minute version. Memorize that version, word for word. Share it with Christian friends to get help in making it as clear and precise as possible.

Next, you need a clear presentation of the plan of salvation. There are tracts available to order on-line that you can use, and this allows you to leave the tract with the person for future reference if needed.

The following are two simple presentations. The Roman Road and one from the Billy Graham Evangelistic Association. Both do require that you have the scripture verses memorized or a small pocket Bible so you can share them with someone else in an easy, well-rehearsed manner.

There are three basic questions to use to start the discussion with someone:

1. Do you have any spiritual beliefs? That is an easy starting point to see where they are and it isn't demanding or accusing like "Do you believe in God?"

2. "If you were to die right now, where do you think you would go?" Regardless of what most people might think, the normal response is, "I'd like to think I would go to heaven."

3. Then it is an easy question to say: If God were to ask you at the pearly gates, "Why should I let you into My heaven?" What would you say?

Sharing Christ with the world or even your next-door neighbor isn't rocket science and it does not require a Bible College or Seminary degree. It just takes someone who is in love with Christ and wants to share what that means to the person next to them.

One of the better books on witnessing is:

Share Jesus Without Fear

by William Fay and Linda Evans Shepherd

B&H Publishing Group 1999

Roman Road Presentation:

Romans 3:23 *"for all have sinned and fall short of the glory of God..."*

Romans 5:8 *"But God demonstrates his own love for us in this: While we were still sinners, Christ died for us."*

Romans 6:23 *"For the wages of sin is death, but the gift of God is eternal life in[a] Christ Jesus our Lord."*

Romans 8:1 *"Therefore, there is now no condemnation for those who are in Christ Jesus."*

Romans 10:9 *"If you declare with your mouth, "Jesus is Lord," and believe in your heart that God raised him from the dead, you will be saved."*

Romans 10:10 *"For it is with your heart that you believe and are justified, and it is with your mouth that you profess your faith and are saved."*

Romans 10:13 *"Everyone who calls on the name of the Lord will be saved."*

You will notice that in pretty much all of the gospel presentation tools you find there are four basic elements: God's Love, Man's Sin, Christ's Death, Our Response. If the presentation you use is missing any one of these elements or adds much more than these, you might want to reevaluate for both simplicity and clarity.

Steps to Peace With God

1. God's Purpose: Peace and Life

God loves you and wants you to experience peace and life—abundant and eternal.

The Bible Says ...

"We have peace with God through our Lord Jesus Christ." *Romans 5:1, NKJV*

"For God so loved the world that He gave His only begotten Son, that whoever believes in Him should not perish but have everlasting life." *John 3:16, NKJV*

"I have come that they may have life, and that they may have it more abundantly." *John 10:10, NKJV*

Since God planned for us to have peace and the abundant life right now, why are most people not having this experience?

2. Our Problem: Separation From God

God created us in His own image to have an abundant life. He did not make us as robots to automatically love and obey Him, but gave us a will and a freedom of choice.

We chose to disobey God and go our own willful way. We still make this choice today. This results in separation from God.

The Bible Says ...

"For all have sinned and fall short of the glory of God." *Romans 3:23, NKJV*

"For the wages of sin is death, but the gift of God is eternal life in Christ Jesus our Lord." *Romans 6:23, NKJV*

Our choice results in separation from God.

People (Sinful)

God (Holy)

Our Attempts

Through the ages, individuals have tried in many ways to bridge this gap ... without success ...

The Bible Says ...

"There is a way that seems right to a man, but its end is the way of death."
Proverbs 14:12, NKJV

"But your iniquities have separated you from your God; and your sins have hidden His face from you, so that He will not hear."
Isaiah 59:2, NKJV

There is only one remedy for this problem of separation.

3. God's Remedy: The Cross

Jesus Christ is the only answer to this problem. He died on the cross and rose from the grave, paying the penalty for our sin and bridging the gap between God and people.

The Bible Says ...

"For there is one God and one Mediator between God and men, the Man Christ Jesus."
1 Timothy 2:5, NKJV

"For Christ also suffered once for sins, the just for the unjust, that He might bring us to God."
1 Peter 3:18, NKJV

"But God shows his love for us in that while we were still sinners, Christ died for us." *Romans 5:8, ESV*

God has provided the only way ... we must make the choice ...

65

4. OUR RESPONSE: RECEIVE CHRIST

We must trust Jesus Christ and receive Him by personal invitation.

THE BIBLE SAYS ...

"Behold, I stand at the door and knock. If anyone hears My voice and opens the door, I will come in to him and dine with him, and he with Me." *Revelation 3:20, NKJV*

"But to all who did receive him, who believed in his name, he gave the right to become children of God." *John 1:12, ESV*

"If you confess with your mouth that Jesus is Lord and believe in your heart that God raised him from the dead, you will be saved." *Romans 10:9, ESV*

Are you here ... or here?

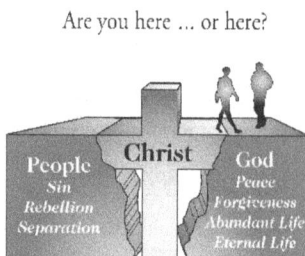

People
Sin
Rebellion
Separation

Christ

God
Peace
Forgiveness
Abundant Life
Eternal Life

Is there any good reason why you cannot receive Jesus Christ right now?

HOW TO RECEIVE CHRIST:

1. Admit your need (say, "I am a sinner").
2. Be willing to turn from your sins (repent) and ask for God's forgiveness.
3. Believe that Jesus Christ died for you on the cross and rose from the grave.
4. Through prayer, invite Jesus Christ to come in and control your life through the Holy Spirit (receive Jesus as Lord and Savior).

WHAT TO PRAY:

> Dear God,
>   I know that I am a sinner. I want to turn from my sins, and I ask for Your forgiveness. I believe that Jesus Christ is Your Son. I believe He died for my sins and that You raised Him to life. I want Him to come into my heart and to take control of my life. I want to trust Jesus as my Savior and follow Him as my Lord from this day forward.
>   In Jesus' Name, amen.
>
> _____   _____
> Date   Signature

Write down the date and time you prayed this prayer and a short description of the details that led you to this important decision:

The Second Coming Of Christ
2 Peter 1:16

I.   What is the Second Coming of Christ?

a. It begins with the "rapture" (removal) of Christians living at that moment on earth – our blessed hope (Titus 2:13; 1 Cor 15:58) as well as all those who have died as Christians over the centuries coming back to meet together in the sky (1 Thess 4:13-18).

   i.   Condition of the world at the time of the rapture:

      1. Evil reigns as it did in the days of Noah (Matt 24:37-38)
      2. Scoffers question Christ's return (2 Peter 3:3-4; Jude 17-19)
      3. Many fall away (2 Thess 2:1-3a)
      4. Antichrist is revealed (2 Thess 2:3b) – one who proclaims world peace for 3 ½ years, so gaining the world's trust, only to become its dictator and demand to be worshipped as God (Rev 13:1-4; 12:13-17)

   ii.   The occurrence of the rapture (1 Thess 4:15-17)

      1. The Lord descends from heaven with a shout with the voice of the archangel and the trumpet of God (Acts 1:11)
      2. The dead in Christ rise first (1 Cor 15:52)

3. Those who are alive (believers) meet them in the clouds and all believers then meet the Lord in the air (Mark 13:27; Matt 24:40)

iii. The results of the rapture:

1. We will see Jesus as He is and be like Him (1 John 3:2; 1 Cor 15:51-53; Phil 3:20-21)
2. He removes us from the presence of sin (Heb 9:28; 1 Cor 15:54-57)
3. And then we ever be with the Lord (1 Thess 4:17b; John 14:3; Col 3:4)
4. Jesus refreshes those who arrive (Luke 12:37,38)

b. It proceeds with the physical return of Jesus Christ to the earth (Job 19:25-27)

i. Condition of the world after His return and the Church is removed by Him.

1. Satan heals the beast of a fatal head wound and gives him power, throne, and authority to amaze and deceive the world into following him (Rev 13:1-4)

2. The beast blasphemes God and wages war on all who have believed in Christ after the rapture (Rev 13:5-8). There will be those who come to salvation after all Christians have been taken off the earth by Christ and they will remain here.

3. A false prophet arises to help the beast by persuading (by signs) the world to worship the beast and kill all who refuse the mark of the beast, which one has to have in order to buy and sell goods (Rev 13:11-18)

4. A remnant of Israel (144,000) are redeemed (Rev 14:1-16)

5. God pours out seven plagues on the earth (Rev 15:5-8; Luke 21:25-26)

6. All the kings of the earth give their power and authority to the beast to wage war (Rev 17:12-14)

ii. The occurrence of Christ's return (2 Thess 1:7-10)

1. Christ appears to the entire world (Rev 19:11-16)

2. The saints follow him in the clouds (Rev 19:14)

3. The Lord comes with Power and great Glory (Matt 16:27; 25:31; Luke 9:26; 21:27; Jude 14-15)

4. All men, dead and alive see Him coming and wail (Rev 1:7)

5. The beast and the kings of the earth and the armies assemble to make war against the Lord and His army (Rev 19:19)

iii. The results of Christ's return

1. The beast and false prophet are seized and thrown alive into the lake of fire – all the rest are killed with the sword of the Lord (Rev 19:20,21; 2 Thess 2:8)

2. An angel binds up the devil (the dragon) and throws him into the abyss and seals it for 1,000 years (Rev 20:1-3a)

3. The saints reign and those who were killed in the tribulation are raised again to reign with Christ. The Millennium begins (Rev 20:4-6)

4. After 1,000 years Satan is released one last time to lead the final war against the reigning saints in Jerusalem (Rev 20:7-9a)

5. The devil and his army are defeated – he is thrown into the lake of fire (Rev 20:9-10)

6. The great white throne of judgment of all non-believers begins as the heavens and the earth are destroyed – all non-believers are thrown into the lake of fire (Rev 20:5, 20:11-15; 2 Peter 3:10)

7. Believer's works are tested by fire and rewards are given (1 Peter 5:4; 1 Cor 3:11-15; 1 Tim 4:8)

8. God creates a new heaven and a new earth – God dwells with His people in perfect peace (Rev 21-22; Isa 65:17-25; Zeph 3:11-13)

II. How are we to prepare for Christ's return?

    a. Watch for His coming (Luke 12:35-40)

    b. Be holy in conduct (1 Tim 6:13-15; 2 Peter 3:11-14; 1 John 3:3; Luke12:35-36)

    c. Be patient (James 5:7-9)

    d. Rejoice in suffering as a trial of your faith (James 1:2-4; 1 Peter 4:13; 1:7; Rev 3:11)

    e. Abide (Live) in Christ (1 John 2:28)

    f. Do not be ashamed of Christ or his Word (Luke 9:26)

    g. Hope in His coming (1 Peter 1:13)

    h. Invest your life in people (1 Thess 2:19)

    i. Comfort one another with these words (1 Thess 4:18; 5:11)

There are a great many word pictures in the book of Revelation because John was trying to describe in human terms of his era all that he had seen in the vision from God in order that believers he was writing to might be able to understand and relate to what he experienced. If you were transported from that era into our current time and had to write about the initial "Shock And Awe" battles staged by the US forces in the first days of the Iraqi war, how would you describe the missiles, jets, helicopters, tanks and violent noise of battle? Symbolism does not compromise what he is describing from reality or the truth of the carnage to come when Christ returns. Christ's return will be as God showed John and the return for Christians will be more glorious and powerful than we can ever imagine. Those who have rejected Christ's offer of salvation will be so overcome by what is happening that they will try to hide and even crawl under rocks to escape (Rev 6:15-17).

Promises

Regarding promises found in scripture, Charles Swindoll in his book "Elijah A Man of Heroism and Humanity" has dedicated part of chapter six "A Promise of God" to a warning about claiming some promises in scripture and it is worth reading. In a simplified summary Rev. Swindoll points out that not all promises in the Bible are for us today. Some were meant for a unique situation and given to a specific person or group of individuals in the days in which Scripture was being lived out. These promises would only have applied in that situation and to that person or people. Other promises are general in nature and have a much broader-based universal appeal and application. Here again, the reader must look at the context of the scripture verse(s) and chapter(s) to determine if this is a specific promise to that person or people or if it is a universal promise to everyone. It is unwise to claim specific promises that were meant for another time, person or group. An example of a specific promise to a specific person or group is Joshua 6 regarding marching around the city of Jericho or Mark 16:18 regarding picking up snakes or drinking deadly poison. It is not appropriate to claim a promise out of its context in Scripture, apart from its primary setting and away from its original meaning. If it is a promise in a unique situation to a specific Biblical character then it is presented in Scripture as an example of how God can work in the lives of His people rather than being a general promise for all His people to claim or expect.

Universal promises abound in scripture and can be claimed without question. Some of these noted in Swindoll's book include Psalms 103:11-13, Proverbs 3:5-6, Isaiah 41:10, Romans 10:11-13, Philippians 4:19, 1 Thessalonians 4:16-17 and 1 Peter 4:12-17.

Also noted in Swindoll's book is the fact that some promises are conditional, meaning they require us to do something in order to receive the promise. 1 John 1:9 is a conditional promise "If we confess our sins, He is faithful and just and will forgive us our sins and purify us from all unrighteousness."(NIV) Until we do our part by confessing sin, we cannot expect the promise of forgiveness or cleansing.

Other promises are unconditional such as "Your word is a lamp to my feet, And a light to my path." Psalm 119:105 "And my God will supply all your needs according to His riches in glory in Christ Jesus" Philippians 4:19. This type requires only that you claim the promise and believe in faith that what God has said is true.

I. What are the promises of God?

 a. That which is true and will be fulfilled:

    i. Because they are based on His character and
       faithfulness (2 Cor 1:19-20, Josh 21:45; Num 23:19)
    ii. According to His timetable (2 Peter 2:8-9; Acts 7:17)
    iii. In His way (Heb 11:13; Gen 17:17,19; 21:1-3)

b. Kinds of promises:

   i. Biblical Evidence. These are promises that were given to a specific person or people at a specific time in Scripture for a particular need or event (Josh 6; Mark 16:18). They show us that God gives promises and fulfills them.

   ii. General: those given to all believers

      1. Conditional, if you do this, I will do this (1 John 1:9; Eph 6:1-3; Matt 21:22)

      2. Unconditional (Luke 12:11-12; Heb 9:27-28)

   iii. Specific: those given uniquely to an individual believer to guide him (Gen 12:1-3)

II. Why we need the promises of God:

   a. To help us escape from the corruption of the world (2 Peter 1:4)

   b. To enable us to partake of His divine nature (2 Peter 1:4)

   c. To give us hope (Heb 10:23)

   d. To motivate us to holy living (2 Cor 7:1; 2 Peter 3:11-14)

   e. To build up and establish our faith (Heb 11:11-12; 11:17-19)

   f. To reveal to us and give us our inheritance (Gal 3:29; Rom 4:16; 8:17)

   g. To guide us (Heb 11:7; Gen 6:8-22)

III. How do we know and claim the promises of God?

   a. Find out the promises of God through reading and study of His Word (Ps 119:148)

i. For general promises:

1. Look for general promises as you regularly read God's Word (Deut 32:46-47; John 6:63). Start a list and record them as you come upon them.

2. As you discover God's promises to every believer, claim them as your own and stand on them.

ii. For specific promises:

1. Recognize your need before God for a specific direction from Him (1 Sam 30:7-8; Judges 6:36-40)

2. ***Don't Hunt***! Ask God to give it as you continue to read regularly in God's Word (Ps 1:2; 27:14)

3. When you believe God has spoken to you, ask God for confirmation and to not allow you to misinterpret His promise (Judge 6:11-40)

iii. Moving forward:

1. Claim the promise, memorize the scripture and meditate on it. Write down your impressions from these verses in your journal

2. Have faith (Heb 11:6; 10:36)

   a. Believe it to be so (Heb 6:12)
   b. Act as if it were already so (Heb 6:12-13)

3. Patiently wait for God to fulfill it (Heb 6:12; 10:36; Ps 119:140)

4. Ask God to guide you further with more insight into Scripture and more promises. (Ps 119:18)

Personal Holiness

Personal holiness is a work of gradual development in a Christian. It is carried on under many hindrances from the world around us and even principalities and powers of the devil (Eph 6:10-12), hence the frequent admonitions in Scripture to watchfulness, prayer, and perseverance (Col 4:2; 1 Peter 5:8-9)

I.   What is personal holiness?

   a. The work of the Triune God (Father, Son, Holy Spirit) in the lives of Christians (1 Thess 5:23; Ex 31:13; Eph 1:4)

   b. The resolute, willful decision of man (2 Tim 2:20-21)

      A. Blamelessness before God (1Thess 3:13; Titus 1:7)

      B. Recognizing our position as priests before God (1 Peter 2:9; Ex 19:6a)

         1. Ordained – Called by God Himself (2 Cor 1:21-22)

         2. Consecrated – Set apart (John 17:18-19; Ex 29:44)

            a. Dedicated to God (Rom 12:1)
            b. Separated from the world (John 15:19; Ps 4:3; Lev 10:10; 20:26)

II. Why we need personal holiness:

a. The Almighty God commands it (Rom 12:1; Matt 5:48; Gen 17:1; Lev 11:44-45)

b. God has chosen us for it (Eph 1:4; Deut 14:2; 26:19)

c. We cannot stand before our enemies without it (Josh 7:11-13)

d. We cannot stand in God's presence without it (Ps 24:3-4)

e. It brings us God's blessings (Deut 11:22-25; 2 Chron 7:13,14)

f. We cannot be satisfied in life without it (Rom 12:1-2)

g. It is necessary to serve Him without fear (Luke 1:74-75)

h. We are God's temple and His Spirit dwells in us (1 Cor 3:16; 6:19-20)

i. God destroys those who are not holy (1 Cor 3:16-17; Acts 5:1-11)

j. It reveals our relationship with God (2 Cor 7:1; Eph 4:22-24; 2 Tim 2:19-21a; 1 Thess 4:7-8)

k. We are unfit for God to use us without it (2 Tim 2:21a)

l. We cannot love without it (1 Tim 1:5)

m. It is necessary preparation to do good works (2 Tim 2:21c)

n. We cannot see God without it (Matt 5:8; Heb 12:14)

o. It reveals our obedience (1 Peter 1:14-16)

p. It is necessary to become a spiritual leader to your family and others (Titus 1:7)

q. It reveals our hope and perspective (2 Peter 3:11-14; Titus 1:15a; 1 John 3:3; 1 Peter 1:13-16)

r. We are hypocrites without it (Rev 3:1-3; 1 John 2:4-6)
    Saying we are what we are not

III. How to become a holy person:

Become a Christian (Col 1:21-22; Acts 26:17b-18)

Keep all know sin confessed (1 John 1:9)

Cooperate with God in your sanctification (2 Tim 2:21) –

Sanctification involves more than a mere moral reformation of character, brought about by the power of the truth: it is the work of the Holy Spirit bringing the whole nature more and more under the influences of the new gracious principles implanted in the soul in regeneration (salvation). In other words, sanctification is the carrying on to perfection the work begun in accepting Christ as savior and Lord, and it extends to the whole man (Romans 6:13-14; 2 Corinthians 4:6; Colossians 3:10; 1 Corinthians 6:19-20). It is the special duty of the Holy Spirit in the plan of redemption to carry on this work (1 Corinthians 6:11; 2 Thessalonians 2:13-14). Faith is instrumental in securing sanctification, inasmuch as it (1) secures union to Christ (Galatians 2:20), and (2) brings the believer into living contact with the truth, whereby "faith accepts each particular passage as to understand and use it in accordance with its evident intention – if an command obeying it; if a *warning*, taking warning by it; if a promise, laying hold on it. And applying it either to this life or to the future life, as a fair interpretation requires."*

---

*Handbooks For Bible Classes, Westminster Confession of Faith, notes by Rev J MacPherson. Edinburgh T&T Clark 1881, Of Saving Faith, page 99.

A. Dedicate yourself to God – commit every area of your life to the Lordship of Jesus Christ beginning with the most important and precious areas of your life (Body Rom 12:1; Possessions Phil 3:8; Self-importance John 13:12-17)

B. Separate yourself from the world – commit yourself to obey, and actually obey, God instead of the world (2 Cor 7:1; 1 Peter 1:14-16; Deut 28:9; Gal 1:10; Eph 2:1-10)

1. Avoid any form of evil (sin) (1 Cor 6:18-20; 2 Cor 6:14-17; 1 Thess 4:3-7; 5:5; 5:22; 2 Tim 2:20-21; Eph 4:25-32)

2. Abhor evil and actively pursue righteousness (Rom 12:9; 2 Tim 2:22; 1 Tim 4:12; 6:11-12; 1 Peter 1:22)

3. Walk by the Spirit (Gal 5:16-25; Rom 8:13; 15:13)

4. Be under God's spiritual disciplines (Heb 12:10), especially that of transforming your mind through the Word of God (Eph 4:20-24; John 17:17; Ps 119:129-130; Prov 2:1-8)

5. Hope in Christ's return (2 Peter 3:11-14; Titus 2:13-14; 1 John 3:2-3)

See study on "The Second Coming of Christ" above.

Names of God

The list below is courtesy of https://newcreeations.org.

Elohim
(God)

First seen in Genesis 1:1 – Used 2599 times in the Bible

This is the very first name given to God found in the very first verse of Genesis. This name shows that God is the majestic ruler over all. Elohim is actually a plural word and its use as the first name of God and sets him high above all other gods. It also foreshadows the later revelation of the triune Godhead – Father, Son, and Holy Spirit.

Yahweh
(Lord, Jehovah)

First seen in Genesis 2:4 – Used 6519 times in the Bible

Yahweh is the promised proper name of God. It means *Lord and Master*. By Jewish tradition, this name is too holy to pronounce or write. Therefore, they just wrote four letters without any vowels: YHWH. Jews stopped saying the name altogether in the third century AD. They stopped saying this name because they were afraid of violating the fourth commandment that prohibits misusing or taking the Lord's name in vain. Therefore, scholars, today don't know for sure if the original pronunciation was Yahweh or Jehovah.

Tradition follows the convention used in the King James Version which translates YHWH by itself as LORD with a capital L and small capital letters for the rest of the word. This is done to set it apart from other uses of the word lord. Then whenever YHWH occurs as a compound name with other words the translators use the word Jehovah instead.

El Elyon
(The Most High God)

First seen in Genesis 14:18 – Used 52 times in the Bible (sometimes without El, simply as Elyon)

El is likely related to the word Elohim and is used in conjunction with other descriptive words to specifically reference a particular characteristic of God. Elyon means highest or most high. Used together El Elyon means *The Most High God*. It refers to the characteristic of God that is above everyone and everything. This name describes his position as sovereign majestic preeminent God.

Adonai
(Lord, Master)

First seen in Genesis 15:2 – Used 434 times in the Bible

Because the Jews have a tradition of not pronouncing nor spelling out the promised proper name of God they often would use Adonai instead of YHWH. Adonai means *Lord*, *Master*, or *Owner*. This name emphasizes that God is in charge of his creation and his people, Lord of lords.

El Shaddai
(Lord God Almighty)

First seen in Genesis 17:1 – Used 48 times in the Bible (sometimes without El, simply as Shaddai)

El is likely related to the word Elohim and is used in conjunction with other descriptive words to specifically reference a particular characteristic of God. Shaddai derives from the word for a woman's breast (*shad*) and literally means "many breasted one." This denotes God as the provider, supplying, nourishing, and satisfying his people with their needs as a mother would her child. God our sustainer.

Shaddai is also related to the Hebrew word *shadad* which means to overpower or destroy, referring to God's absolute power. This describes God as the one who triumphs over every obstacle and all opposition.

Used together El Shaddai is usually translated *Lord God Almighty*. God is our all-powerful and all-sufficient sustainer.

El Olam
(The Everlasting God)

First seen in Genesis 21:33 – Used 439 times in the Bible

El is likely related to the word Elohim and is used in conjunction with other descriptive words to specifically reference a particular characteristic of God. Olam means forever, always, continuous existence, perpetual, everlasting, evermore, perpetual, indefinite or unending future, eternity. Used together El Olam means *The Everlasting God*. He exists beyond time and space. We can take comfort in the fact that God always was, and always will be God. Nothing we can ever face will change that because God is unchangeable.

Jehovah Jireh
(The LORD Will Provide)

Only occurs once in Genesis 22:14

Jehovah is actually YHWH (see Yahweh above) and means Lord and Master. It is the promised and proper name of God. Jireh means to see or provide. When Isaac asked Abraham where the lamb was for the sacrifice, Abraham replied that the Lord would provide. After God provided the ram for the sacrifice Abraham named that place on Mount Moriah Jehovah Jireh, meaning *The LORD Will Provide*. God is quietly arranging things behind the scenes so that they will be in just the right place exactly when we need them.

Jehovah Rapha
(The LORD Who Heals You)

Occurs only once in Exodus 15:26

Jehovah is actually YHWH (see Yahweh above) and means Lord and Master. It is the promised and proper name of God. Rapha means to heal or make healthful. Together, Jehovah Rapha means *The LORD Who Heals You*. God is the Great Physician who heals his people. This truth in God's name applies equally to emotional, psychological, and physical healing as well as to nations and individuals alike.

Jehovah Nissi
(The LORD Is My Banner)

Occurs only once in Exodus 17:15

Jehovah is actually YHWH (see Yahweh above) and means Lord and Master. It is the promised and proper name of God. Nissi means flag or banner so together Jehovah Nissi means *The LORD Is My Banner*. God himself is our banner and victory. He gives us hope and a focus and is the one who wins our battles.

El Qanna
(Jealous God)

First seen in Exodus 20:5 – Used 6 times in 5 verses in the Bible

El is likely related to the word Elohim and is used in conjunction with other descriptive words to specifically reference a particular characteristic of God. Qanna means jealous, zealous, or envy. Used together El Qanna means *Jealous God*. God's jealousy is a holy, loving jealousy without any of the insecure manipulation or control that comes packaged with worldly jealousy. It draws from the marriage relationship with a picture of a husband jealous for his wife. God longs for each of us to put Him first in our lives in priority and importance, not out of ego, but because he knows that is Him what is best for us. Ex 20:5; Ex 34:14; Deu 4:24; Deu 5:9; Deu 6:15

Jehovah Mekoddishkem
(The LORD Who Sanctifies You)

First seen in Exodus 31:13 (Only other occurrence is in Leviticus 20:8)

Jehovah is actually YHWH (see Yahweh above) and means Lord and Master. It is the promised and proper name of God. Mekoddishkem means holy or set apart. It is the process of sanctification, which is the separation of something so that it is holy. Used together Jehovah Mekoddishkem (can have the variant spelling Jehovah M'Kaddesh) means *The LORD Who Sanctifies You*. God sets us apart as his children when we become believers. He sanctifies us and makes us holy because we are incapable of it on our own.

Jehovah Shalom
(The LORD Is Peace)

Occurs only once in Judges 6:24

Jehovah is actually YHWH (see Yahweh above) and means Lord and Master. It is the promised and proper name of God. Shalom means peace, absence of strife, complete, or sound. Used together Jehovah Shalom means *The LORD Is Peace.* When it seems like the whole world is against you or that you are completely unable to deal with whatever problem is in front of you, turn to the God of peace to find comfort and strength.

Jehovah Sabaoth
(The LORD of Hosts)

First seen in 1 Samuel 1:3 – Used in the Bible more than 285 times

Jehovah is actually YHWH (see Yahweh above) and means Lord and Master. It is the promised and proper name of God. Sabaoth means an army going out to war. Used together Jehovah Sabaoth means *The LORD of Armies* or *The LORD of Hosts.* The Lord reigns over a vast well-ordered host in the heavenlies. God is always there to defend us, fight our battles, and win our wars. There is no enemy He cannot defeat.

Jehovah Raah
(The Lord Is My Shepherd)

Occurs once in Psalms 23:1. (Raah is also used in reference to God in Genesis 48:15, Genesis 49:24, and Psalm 80:1)

Jehovah is actually YHWH (see Yahweh above) and means Lord and Master. It is the promised and proper name of God. Raah means to shepherd or feed, to supply with food, and to be a good friend. Jehovah Raah means *The Lord Is My Shepherd*. God is a friend who provides extravagant nourishment, protection, as well as rest for our weary bodies and souls.

Jehovah Tsidkenu
(The Lord Our Righteousness)

First seen in Jeremiah 23:6 – Only other occurrence is in Jeremiah 33:16

Jehovah is actually YHWH (see Yahweh above) and means Lord and Master. It is the promised and proper name of God. Tsidkenu means justice, rightness, righteousness, deliverance, victory, and prosperity. Used together Jehovah Tsidkenu means *The LORD Who Is Our Righteousness*. God himself stands for us and provides us with His righteousness and justice when we don't have any in ourselves. He is the one who provides victory and prosperity.

Jehovah Shammah
(The LORD Is There)

Occurs only once in Ezekiel 48:35

Jehovah is actually YHWH (see Yahweh above) and
means Lord and Master. It is the promised and proper
name of God. Shammah is an adverb that simply
means *there*, although when it's used in relation to time
it means *then*. Together Jehovah Shammah means *The
LORD is There*. God revealed this name at a time when
Israel was in rebellion and in captivity. God was letting
the Jews know that he had not forsaken them and that
He was still there, both in their present as well as in their
future. Regardless of what you are going through, or
what you are heading into, you can take comfort
knowing that God is already there.

All The Names of Jesus

Courtesy of Christ Unlimited Ministries
– http://BibleResources.org

The following list is of names and titles given specifically to our Lord Jesus. The more we study this list, the more we will understand who Jesus really is. How can we help but love Him?

All Scriptures are taken from the King James Version of the Bible.

ADAM: (1 Corinthians 15:45) And so it is written, The first man Adam was made a living soul; the last Adam was made a quickening spirit.

ADVOCATE: (1 John 2:1) My little children, these things write I unto you, that ye sin not. And if any man sin, we have an advocate with the Father, Jesus Christ the righteous:

ALMIGHTY: (Revelation 1:8) I am Alpha and Omega, the beginning and the ending, saith the Lord, which is, and which was, and which is to come, the Almighty.

ALPHA AND OMEGA:
(Revelation 1:8) I am Alpha and Omega, the beginning and the ending, saith the Lord, which is, and which was, and which is to come, the Almighty.

AMEN: (Revelation 3:14) And unto the angel of the church of the Laodiceans write; These things saith the Amen, the faithful and true witness, the beginning of the creation of God;

APOSTLE OF OUR PROFESSION:
(Hebrews 3:1) Wherefore, holy brethren, partakers of the heavenly calling, consider the Apostle and High Priest of our profession, Christ Jesus;

ARM OF THE LORD: (Isaiah 51:9) Awake, awake, put on strength, O arm of the LORD; awake, as in the ancient days, in the generations of old. Art thou not it that hath cut Rahab, and wounded the dragon? (Isaiah 53:1) Who hath believed our report? and to whom is the arm of the LORD revealed?

AUTHOR AND FINISHER OF OUR FAITH:
(Hebrews 12:2) Looking unto Jesus the author and finisher of our faith; who for the joy that was set before him endured the cross, despising the shame, and is set down at the right hand of the throne of God.

AUTHOR OF ETERNAL SALVATION: (Hebrews 5:9) And being made perfect, he became the author of eternal salvation unto all them that obey him;

BEGINNING OF CREATION OF GOD (Revelation 3:14) And unto the angel of the church of the Laodiceans write; These things saith the Amen, the faithful and true witness, the beginning of the creation of God;

BELOVED SON: (Matthew 12:18) Behold my servant, whom I have chosen; my beloved, in whom my soul is well pleased: I will put my spirit upon him, and he shall show judgment to the Gentiles;

BLESSED AND ONLY POTENTATE: (1 Timothy 6:15) Which in his times he shall show, who is the blessed and only Potentate, the King of kings, and Lord of lords;

BRANCH: (Isaiah 4:2) In that day shall the branch of the LORD be beautiful and glorious, and the fruit of the earth shall be excellent and comely for them that are escaped of Israel.

BREAD OF LIFE: (John 6:32) Then Jesus said unto them, Verily, verily, I say unto you, Moses gave you not that bread from heaven; but my Father giveth you the true bread from heaven.

CAPTAIN OF SALVATION:
(Hebrews 2:10) For it became him, for whom are all things, and by whom are all things, in bringing many sons unto glory, to make the captain of their salvation perfect through sufferings.

CHIEF SHEPHERD: (1 Peter 5:4) And when the chief Shepherd shall appear, ye shall receive a crown of glory that fadeth not away.

CHRIST OF GOD: (Luke 9:20) He said unto them, But whom say ye that I am? Peter answering said, The Christ of God.

CONSOLATION OF ISRAEL:
(Luke 2:25) And, behold, there was a man in Jerusalem, whose name was Simeon; and the same man was just and devout, waiting for the consolation of Israel: and the Holy Ghost was upon him.

CORNERSTONE: (Psalm 118:22) The stone which the builders refused is become the head stone of the corner.

COUNSELLOR: (Isaiah 9:6) For unto us a child is born, unto us a son is given: and the government shall be upon his shoulder: and his name shall be called Wonderful, Counsellor, The mighty God, The everlasting Father, The Prince of Peace.

CREATOR: (John 1:3) All things were made by him; and without him was not anything made that was made.

DAYSPRING: (Luke 1:78) Through the tender mercy of our God; whereby the dayspring from on high hath visited us,

DELIVERER: (Romans 11:26) And so all Israel shall be saved: as it is written, There shall come out of Zion the Deliverer, and shall turn away ungodliness from Jacob:

DESIRE OF THE NATIONS:
(Haggai 2:7) And I will shake all nations, and the desire of all nations shall come: and I will fill this house with glory, saith the LORD of hosts.

DOOR: (John 10:7) Then said Jesus unto them again, Verily, verily, I say unto you, I am the door of the sheep.

ELECT OF GOD: (Isaiah 42:1) Behold my servant, whom I uphold; mine elect, in whom my soul delighteth; I have put my spirit upon him: he shall bring forth judgment to the Gentiles.

EVERLASTING FATHER: (Isaiah 9:6) For unto us a child is born, unto us a son is given: and the government shall be upon his shoulder: and his name shall be called Wonderful, Counsellor, The mighty God, The everlasting Father, The Prince of Peace.

FAITHFUL WITNESS:
(Revelation 1:5) And from Jesus Christ, who is the faithful witness, and the first begotten of the dead, and the prince of the kings of the earth. Unto him that loved us, and washed us from our sins in his own blood,

FIRST AND LAST: (Revelation 1:17) And when I saw him, I fell at his feet as dead. And he laid his right hand upon me, saying unto me, Fear not; I am the first and the last:

FIRST BEGOTTEN: (Revelation 1:5) And from Jesus Christ, who is the faithful witness, and the first begotten of the dead, and the prince of the kings of the earth. Unto him that loved us, and washed us from our sins in his own blood,

FORERUNNER: (Hebrews 6:20) Whither the forerunner is for us entered, even Jesus, made an high priest for ever after the order of Melchizedec.

GLORY OF THE LORD: (Isaiah 40:5) And the glory of the LORD shall be revealed, and all flesh shall see it together: for the mouth of the LORD hath spoken it.

GOD: (Isaiah 40:3) The voice of him that crieth in the wilderness, Prepare ye the way of the LORD, make straight in the desert a highway for our God.

GOD BLESSED: (Romans 9:5) Whose are the fathers, and of whom as concerning the flesh Christ came, who is over all, God blessed forever. Amen.

GOOD SHEPHERD: (John 10:11) I am the good shepherd: the good shepherd giveth his life for the sheep.

GOVERNOR: (Matthew 2:6) And thou Bethlehem, in the land of Juda, art not the least among the princes of Juda: for out of thee shall come a Governor, that shall rule my people Israel.

GREAT HIGH PRIEST: (Hebrews 4:14) Seeing then that we have a great high priest, that is passed into the heavens, Jesus the Son of God, let us hold fast our profession.

HEAD OF THE CHURCH:
(Ephesians 1:22) And hath put all things under his feet, and gave him to be the head over all things to the church,

HEIR OF ALL THINGS: (Hebrews 1:2) Hath in these last days spoken unto us by his Son, whom he hath appointed heir of all things, by whom also he made the worlds;

HOLY CHILD: (Acts 4:27) For of a truth against thy holy child Jesus, whom thou hast anointed, both Herod, and Pontius Pilate, with the Gentiles, and the people of Israel, were gathered together,

HOLY ONE: (Acts 3:14) But ye denied the Holy One and the Just, and desired a murderer to be granted unto you;

HOLY ONE OF GOD: (Mark 1:24) Saying, Let us alone; what have we to do with thee, thou Jesus of Nazareth? art thou come to destroy us? I know thee who thou art, the Holy One of God.

HOLY ONE OF ISRAEL: (Isaiah 41:14) Fear not, thou worm Jacob, and ye men of Israel; I will help thee, saith the LORD, and thy redeemer, the Holy One of Israel.

HORN OF SALVATION: (Luke 1:69) And hath raised up an horn of salvation for us in the house of his servant David;

I AM: (John 8:58) Jesus said unto them, Verily, verily, I say unto you, Before Abraham was, I am.

IMAGE OF GOD: (2 Corinthians 4:4) In whom the god of this world hath blinded the minds of them which believe not, lest the light of the glorious gospel of Christ, who is the image of God, should shine unto them.

IMMANUEL: (Isaiah 7:14) Therefore the Lord himself shall give you a sign; Behold, a virgin shall conceive, and bear a son, and shall call his name Immanuel.

JEHOVAH: (Isaiah 26:4) Trust ye in the LORD forever: for in the LORD JEHOVAH is everlasting strength:

JESUS: (Matthew 1:21) And she shall bring forth a son, and thou shalt call his name JESUS: for he shall save his people from their sins.

JESUS OF NAZARETH: (Matthew 21:11) And the multitude said, This is Jesus the prophet of Nazareth of Galilee.

JUDGE OF ISRAEL: (Micah 5:1) Now gather thyself in troops, O daughter of troops: he hath laid siege against us: they shall smite the judge of Israel with a rod upon the cheek.

THE JUST ONE: (Acts 7:52) Which of the prophets have not your fathers persecuted? and they have slain them which showed before of the coming of the Just One; of whom ye have been now the betrayers and murderers:

KING: (Zechariah 9:9) Rejoice greatly, O daughter of Zion; shout, O daughter of Jerusalem: behold, thy King cometh unto thee: he is just, and having salvation; lowly, and riding upon an ass, and upon a colt the foal of an ass.

KING OF THE AGES: (1 Timothy 1:17) Now unto the King eternal, immortal, invisible, the only wise God, be honor and glory for ever and ever. Amen.

KING OF THE JEWS: (Matthew 2:2) Saying, Where is he that is born King of the Jews? for we have seen his star in the east, and are come to worship him.

KING OF KINGS: (1 Timothy 6:15) Which in his times he shall show, who is the blessed and only Potentate, the King of kings, and Lord of lords;

KING OF SAINTS: (Revelation 15:3) And they sing the song of Moses the servant of God, and the song of the Lamb, saying, Great and marvelous are thy works, Lord God Almighty; just and true are thy ways, thou King of saints.

LAWGIVER: (Isaiah 33:22) For the LORD is our judge, the LORD is our lawgiver, the LORD is our king; he will save us.

LAMB: (Revelation 13:8) And all that dwell upon the earth shall worship him, whose names are not written in the book of life of the Lamb slain from the foundation of the world.

LAMB OF GOD: (John 1:29) The next day John seeth Jesus coming unto him, and saith, Behold the Lamb of God, which taketh away the sin of the world.

LEADER AND COMMANDER:
(Isaiah 55:4) Behold, I have given him for a witness to the people, a leader and commander to the people.

THE LIFE: (John 14:6) Jesus saith unto him, I am the way, the truth, and the life: no man cometh unto the Father, but by me.

LIGHT OF THE WORLD: (John 8:12) Then spake Jesus again unto them, saying, I am the light of the world: he that followeth me shall not walk in darkness, but shall have the light of life.

LION OF THE TRIBE OF JUDAH: (Revelation 5:5) And one of the elders saith unto me, Weep not: behold, the Lion of the tribe of Juda, the Root of David, hath prevailed to open the book, and to loose the seven seals thereof.

LORD OF ALL: (Acts 10:36) The word which God sent unto the children of Israel, preaching peace by Jesus Christ: (he is Lord of all:)

LORD OF GLORY: (1 Corinthians 2:8) Which none of the princes of this world knew: for had they known it, they would not have crucified the Lord of glory.

LORD OF LORDS: (1 Timothy 6:15) Which in his times he shall show, who is the blessed and only Potentate, the King of kings, and Lord of lords;

LORD OF OUR RIGHTEOUSNESS:
(Jeremiah 23:6) In his days Judah shall be saved, and Israel shall dwell safely: and this is his name whereby he shall be called, THE LORD OUR RIGHTEOUSNESS.

MAN OF SORROWS: (Isaiah 53:3) He is despised and rejected of men; a man of sorrows, and acquainted with grief: and we hid as it were our faces from him; he was despised, and we esteemed him not.

MEDIATOR: (1 Timothy 2:5) For there is one God, and one mediator between God and men, the man Christ Jesus;

MESSENGER OF THE COVENANT:
(Malachi 3:1) Behold, I will send my messenger, and he shall prepare the way before me: and the Lord, whom ye seek, shall suddenly come to his temple, even the messenger of the covenant, whom ye delight in: behold, he shall come, saith the LORD of hosts.

MESSIAH: (Daniel 9:25) Know therefore and understand, that from the going forth of the commandment to restore and to build Jerusalem unto the Messiah the Prince shall be seven weeks, and threescore and two weeks: the street shall be built again, and the wall, even in troublous times. (John 1:41) He first findeth his own brother Simon, and saith unto him, We have found the Messiah, which is, being interpreted, the Christ.

MIGHTY GOD: (Isaiah 9:6) For unto us a child is born, unto us a son is given: and the government shall be upon his shoulder: and his name shall be called Wonderful,

Counsellor, The mighty God, The everlasting Father, The Prince of Peace.

MIGHTY ONE: (Isaiah 60:16) Thou shalt also suck the milk of the Gentiles, and shalt suck the breast of kings: and thou shalt know that I the LORD am thy Savior and thy Redeemer, the mighty One of Jacob.

MORNING STAR: (Revelation 22:16) I Jesus have sent mine angel to testify unto you these things in the churches. I am the root and the offspring of David, and the bright and morning star.

NAZARENE: (Matthew 2:23) And he came and dwelt in a city called Nazareth: that it might be fulfilled which was spoken by the prophets, He shall be called a Nazarene.

ONLY BEGOTTEN SON: (John 1:18) No man hath seen God at any time; the only begotten Son, which is in the bosom of the Father, he hath declared him.

OUR PASSOVER: (1 Corinthians 5:7) Purge out therefore the old leaven, that ye may be a new lump, as ye are unleavened. For even Christ our passover is sacrificed for us:

PRINCE OF LIFE: (Acts 3:15) And killed the Prince of life, whom God hath raised from the dead; whereof we are witnesses.

PRINCE OF KINGS: (Revelation 1:5) And from Jesus Christ, who is the faithful witness, and the first begotten of the dead, and the prince of the kings of the earth. Unto him that loved us, and washed us from our sins in his own blood,

PRINCE OF PEACE: (Isaiah 9:6) For unto us a child is born, unto us a son is given: and the government shall be upon his shoulder: and his name shall be called Wonderful, Counsellor, The mighty God, The everlasting Father, The Prince of Peace.

PROPHET: (Luke 24:19) And he said unto them, What things? And they said unto him, Concerning Jesus of Nazareth, which was a prophet mighty in deed and word before God and all the people: (Acts 3:22) For Moses truly said unto the fathers, A prophet shall the Lord your God raise up unto you of your brethren, like unto me; him shall ye hear in all things whatsoever he shall say unto you.

REDEEMER: (Job 19:25) For I know that my redeemer liveth, and that he shall stand at the latter day upon the earth:

RESURRECTION AND LIFE:
(John 11:25) Jesus said unto her, I am the resurrection, and the life: he that believeth in me, though he were dead, yet shall he live:

ROCK: (1 Corinthians 10:4) And did all drink the same spiritual drink: for they drank of that spiritual Rock that followed them: and that Rock was Christ.

ROOT OF DAVID: (Revelation 22:16) I Jesus have sent mine angel to testify unto you these things in the churches. I am the root and the offspring of David, and the bright and morning star.

ROSE OF SHARON: (Song of Songs 2:1) I am the rose of Sharon, and the lily of the valleys.

SAVIOR: (Luke 2:11) For unto you is born this day in the city of David a Savior, which is Christ the Lord.

SEED OF WOMAN: (Genesis 3:15) And I will put enmity between thee and the woman, and between thy seed and her seed; it shall bruise thy head, and thou shalt bruise his heel.

SHEPHERD AND BISHOP OF SOULS: (1 Peter 2:25) For ye were as sheep going astray; but are now returned unto the Shepherd and Bishop of your souls.

SHILOH: (Genesis 49:10) The scepter shall not depart from Judah, nor a lawgiver from between his feet, until Shiloh come; and unto him shall the gathering of the people be.

SON OF THE BLESSED: (Mark 14:61) But he held his peace, and answered nothing. Again the high priest asked him, and said unto him, Art thou the Christ, the Son of the Blessed?

SON OF DAVID: (Matthew 1:1) The book of the generation of Jesus Christ, the son of David, the son of Abraham.

SON OF GOD: (Matthew 2:15) And was there until the death of Herod: that it might be fulfilled which was spoken of the Lord by the prophet, saying, Out of Egypt have I called my son.

SON OF THE HIGHEST: (Luke 1:32) He shall be great, and shall be called the Son of the Highest: and the Lord God shall give unto him the throne of his father David.

SUN OF RIGHTEOUSNESS:
(Malachi 4:2) But unto you that fear my name shall the Sun of righteousness arise with healing in his wings; and ye shall go forth, and grow up as calves of the stall.

TRUE LIGHT: (John 1:9) That was the true Light, which lighteth every man that cometh into the world.

TRUE VINE: (John 15:1) I am the true vine, and my Father is the husbandman.

TRUTH: (John 1:14) And the Word was made flesh, and dwelt among us, (and we beheld his glory, the glory as of the only begotten of the Father,) full of grace and truth.

WITNESS: (Isaiah 55:4) Behold, I have given him for a witness to the people, a leader and commander to the people.

WORD: (John 1:1) In the beginning was the Word, and the Word was with God, and the Word was God.

WORD OF GOD: (Revelation 19:13) And he was clothed with a vesture dipped in blood: and his name is called The Word of God.

Names of the Holy Spirit in Scripture

The names of the Holy Spirit in Scripture often refer to His actions, role or function. Prior to the resurrection of Jesus He came upon certain people for specific reasons (Joshua Num 27:18; Othniel Judg 3:10; Gideon Judg 6:34; Samson Judg 13:25, 14:6). After the resurrection, He comes into every believer at conversion (Jn 7:37-39; 1 Jn 4:12-14; Eph 1:13). Jesus referred to Him as "Helper" -- one who comes alongside -- (John 14:16, 26; 15:26; 16:7) and in Isaiah 11:2 He is called the Spirit of Counsel. Other names used for the Holy Spirit include:

1. Spirit of glory (1 Peter 4:14)
2. Lord, The (2 Thessalonians 3:5)
3. God (Acts 5:3-4)
4. Spirit of revelation (Ephesians 1:17)
5. Spirit of the Son (Galatians 4:6)
6. Spirit of God (Genesis 1:2; 1 Cor 2:11; Job 33:4)
7. Eternal Spirit (Hebrews 9:14)
8. Spirit of the Lord (Isaiah 11:2; Acts 5:9)
9. Spirit of wisdom (Isaiah 11:2; Ephesians 1:17)
10. Spirit of counsel (Isaiah 11:2)
11. Spirit of might (Isaiah 11:2)
12. Spirit of understanding (Isaiah 11:2)
13. Spirit of knowledge (Isaiah 11:2)
14. Spirit of the fear of the Lord (Isaiah 11:2)
15. Spirit of judgment (Isaiah 4:4; 28:6)

16. Spirit of burning (Isaiah 4:4)
17. Spirit of the Lord God (Isaiah 61:1)
18. Breath of the Almighty (Job 33:4)
19. Comforter (John 14:16, 26; 15:26)
20. Spirit of truth (John 14:17; 15:26)
21. Power of the Highest (Luke 1:35)
22. Spirit of the Father (Matthew 10:20)
23. Spirit, The (Matthew 4:1; John 3:6; 1 Tim 4:1)
24. Good Spirit (Nehemiah 9:20; Psalms 143:10)
25. Holy Spirit (Ps 51:11; Lk 11:13; Eph 1:13; 4:30)
26. Free *(Willing)* Spirit (Psalm 51:12)
27. Spirit of prophecy (Revelation 19:10)
28. Seven Spirits of God (Revelation 1:4)
29. Spirit of holiness (Romans 1:4)
30. Spirit of adoption (Romans 8:15)
31. Spirit of life (Romans 8:2; Revelation 11:11)
32. Spirit of Christ (Romans 8:9; 1 Peter 1:11)
33. Spirit of grace (Zechariah 12:10; Hebrews 10:29)

Prophecies Concerning Christ.

- As the Son of God — Ps 2:7.
  - † Fulfilled. — Luke 1:32,35.
- As the seed of the woman — Gen 3:15.
  - † Fulfilled. — Gal 4:4.
- As the seed of Abraham — Gen 17:7; 22:18.
  - † Fulfilled. — Gal 3:16.
- As the seed of Isaac — Gen 21:12.
  - † Fulfilled. — Heb 11:17-19.
- As the seed of David — Ps 132:11; Jer 23:5.
  - † Fulfilled. — Acts 13:23; Rom 1:3.
- His coming at a set time — Gen 49:10; Daniel 9:24,25.
  - † Fulfilled. — Luke 2:1.
- His being born a virgin — Isa 7:14.
  - † Fulfilled. — Matt 1:22,23; Luke 2:7.
- His being called Immanuel — Isa 7:14.
  - † Fulfilled. — Matt 1:22,23.
- His being born in Bethlehem of Judea — Mic 5:2.
  - † Fulfilled. - Matt 2:1; Luke 2:4-6.
- Great persons coming to adore him — Ps 72:10.
  - † Fulfilled. — Matt 2:1-11.
- The slaying of the children of Bethlehem — Jer 31:15.
  - † Fulfilled. — Matt 2:16-18.
- His being called out of Egypt — Hos 11:1.
  - † Fulfilled. — Matt 2:15.

- His being preceded by John the Baptist — Isa 40:3; Mal 3:1.
  - † Fulfilled. — Matt 3:1,3; Luke 1:17.
- His being anointed with the Spirit — Ps 45:7; Isa 11:2; 61:1.
  - † Fulfilled. — Matt 3:16; John 3:34; Acts 10:38.
- His being a Prophet like to Moses — Deut 18:15-18.
  - † Fulfilled. — Acts 3:20-22.
- His being a Priest after the order of Melchizedek — Ps 110:4.
  - † Fulfilled. — Heb 5:5,6.
- His entering on his public ministry — Isa 61:1,2.
  - † Fulfilled. — Luke 4:16-21,43.
- His ministry commencing in Galilee — Isa 9:1,2.
  - † Fulfilled. — Matt 4:12-16,23.
- His entering publicly into Jerusalem — Zec 9:9.
  - † Fulfilled. — Matt 21:1-5.
- His coming into the temple — Hag 2:7,9; Mal 3:1.
  - † Fulfilled. — Matt 21:12; Luke 2:27-32; John 2:13-16.
- His poverty — Isa 53:2.
  - † Fulfilled. - Mark 6:3; Luke 9:58.
- His meekness and want of ostentatious — Isa 42:2.
  - † Fulfilled. — Matt 12:15,16,19.
- His tenderness and compassion — Isa 40:11; 42:3.
  - † Fulfilled. — Matt 12:15,20; Heb 4:15.
- His being without guile — Isa 53:9.
  - † Fulfilled. —1 Pet 2:22.

- His zeal — Ps 69:9.
  - † Fulfilled. — John 2:17.
- His preaching by parables — Ps 78:2.
  - † Fulfilled. — Matt 13:34,35.
- His working miracles — Isa 35:5,6.
  - † Fulfilled. — Matt 11:4-6; John 11:47.
- His bearing reproach — Ps 22:6; 69:7,9,20.
  - † Fulfilled. — Rom 15:3.
- His being rejected by his brethren — Ps 69:8; Isa 63:3.
  - † Fulfilled. — John 1:11; 7:3.
- His being a stone of stumbling to the Jews — Isa 8:14.
  - † Fulfilled. — Rom 9:32; 1 Pet 2:8.
- His being hated by the Jews — Ps 69:4; Isa 49:7.
  - † Fulfilled. — John 15:24,25.
- His being rejected by the Jewish rulers — Ps 118:22.
  - † Fulfilled. - Matt 21:42; John 7:48.
- That the Jews and Gentiles should combine against Him — Ps 2:1,2.
  - † Fulfilled. - Luke 23:12; Acts 4:27.
- His being betrayed by a friend — Ps 41:9; 55:12-14.
  - † Fulfilled. — John 13:18,21.
- His disciples forsaking him — Zec 13:7.
  - † Fulfilled. — Matt 26:31,56.
- His being sold for thirty pieces silver — Zec 11:12.
  - † Fulfilled. — Matt 26:15.
- His price being given for the potter's field — Zec 11:13.
  - † Fulfilled. — Matt 27:7.

- The intensity of his sufferings — Ps 22:14,15.
  † Fulfilled. — Luke 22:42,44.
- His sufferings being for others — Isa 53:4-6,12;
  Dan 9:26
  † Fulfilled. — Matt 20:28.
- His patience and silence under suffering — Isa 53:7.
  † Fulfilled. - Matt 26:63; 27:12-14.
- His being smitten on the cheek — Mic 5:1.
  † Fulfilled. — Matt 27:30.
- His visage being marred — Isa 52:14; 53:3.
  † Fulfilled. — John 19:5.
- His being spit on and scourged — Isa 50:6.
  † Fulfilled. — Mark 14:65; John 19:1.
- His hands and feet being nailed to the cross —
  Ps 22:16.
  † Fulfilled. — John 19:18; 20:25.
- His being forsaken by God — Ps 22:1.
  † Fulfilled. — Matt 27:46.
- His being mocked — Ps 22:7,8.
  † Fulfilled. — Matt 27:39-44.
- Gall and vinegar being given him to drink —
  Ps 69:21.
  † Fulfilled. — Matt 27:34.
- His garments being parted, and lots cast for his vesture
  Ps 22:18.
  † Fulfilled. — Matt 27:35.

- His being numbered with the transgressors — Isa 53:12.
  - † Fulfilled. — Mark 15:28.
- His intercession for His murderers — Isa 53:12.
  - † Fulfilled. — Luke 23:34.
- His Death — Isa 53:12.
  - † Fulfilled. — Matt 27:50.
- That a bone of him should not be broken — Ex 12:46; Ps 34:20.
  - † Fulfilled. — John 19:33,36.
- His being pierced — Zec 12:10.
  - † Fulfilled. — John 19:34,37.
- His being buried with the rich — Isa 53:9.
  - † Fulfilled. — Matt 27:57-60.
- His flesh not seeing corruption — Ps 16:10.
  - † Fulfilled. — Acts 2:31.
- His resurrection — Ps 16:10; Isa 26:19.
  - † Fulfilled. — Luke 24:6,31,34.
- His ascension — Ps 68:18.
  - † Fulfilled. — Luke 24:51; Acts 1:9.
- His sitting on the right hand of God — Ps 110:1.
  - † Fulfilled. — Heb 1:3.
- His exercising the priestly duties in heaven — Zec 6:13.
  - † Fulfilled. — Rom 8:34.
- His being the chief corner-stone of the Church — Isa 28:16.
  - † Fulfilled. — 1 Pet 2:6,7.

- His being King in Zion — Ps 2:6.
  † Fulfilled. — Luke 1:32; John 18:33-37.

- The conversion of the Gentiles to him — Isa 11:10; Isa 42:1.
  † Fulfilled. — Matt 1:17,21; John 10:16; Acts 10:45,47.

- His righteous government — Ps 45:6,7.
  † Fulfilled. — John 5:30; Rev 19:11.

- His universal dominion — Ps 72:8; Daniel 7:14.
  † Fulfilled. — Phil 2:9,11.

- The perpetuity of his kingdom — Isa 9:7; Daniel 7:14.
  † Fulfilled. — Luke 1:32,33.

Basics on Cult Religions

The three most common teachings of Christian cults are that Jesus was not God, that salvation is not by faith alone and man is not sinful (separated from God). These beliefs are in direct opposition to the Bible which required these cults to rewrite the Bible or substitute some other book for or in addition to the Bible.

There are many religions in the world today just as there has been from the beginning of time itself. None of those religions offer enduring peace, fulfillment and forgiveness like Christianity. Most of those religions can be easy to spot such as Hinduism, Buddhist, even Islam but a few attempt to hide behind a sham of Christianity. Mormonism (Church of the Latter-Day Saints), the Church of Scientology and the Jehovah Witnesses are illustrations. Although there are many "good" people in these organizations who genuinely believe they hold the truth, the "truth" they hold does not stand the test of scripture.

Walter Martin, in "The Rise of the Cults"(Vision House Pub), page 12, gives us a good definition of a cult when he says:

A cult, then, is a group of people polarized around someone's interpretation of the Bible and is characterized by major deviations from orthodox Christianity relative to the cardinal doctrines of the Christian faith, particularly the fact that God became man in Jesus Christ.

Even in the garden of Eden, these cults had their start when Satan asked Eve, "Has God said? You won't die. Take a bite and become like God." The death Adam and Eve suffered was not immediate death and the grave but rather an immediate death of separation from the God who loved them and created them. This barrier continued to be inherited by every one of their descendants until Jesus came, born of a virgin (without original sin in Him), lived a sinless life, died on the Roman cross as a sacrifice for the sin of mankind, buried and rose again on the third day ascending into heaven. We now have access to God and eternal life with Him by accepting what Christ did for us as payment for our sin and accepting Him into our hearts as Lord and Savior.

The first thing that you will see when you encounter a false religion hiding behind Christianity is that they question God's Word and put some other book or person before it as their holy scripture and prophet. This was evident even in the years immediately following Christ's resurrection.

Peter writes in 2 Peter 1:20,21: *"But I know this first of all, that no prophecy of Scripture is a matter of one's own interpretation, for no prophecy was ever made by an act of human will, but men moved by the Holy Spirit spoke from God."* Peter then goes on in chapter two to warn of false teachers. Proverbs 30:5,6 states *"Every word of God is tested; He is a shield to those who take refuge in Him. Do not add to His words or He will reprove you, and you will be proved a liar."* John in the final part of Revelation in

22:18 states, "*I testify to everyone who hears the words of the prophecy of this book: if anyone adds to them, God will add to him the plagues which are written in this book: and if anyone takes away from the words of the book of this prophecy, God will take away his part from the tree of life and from the holy city, which is written in this book.*" The apostle Paul was very specific about anyone trying to add to or adulterate the Gospel of Jesus Christ. In Galatians 1:6-9 he writes, "*I am amazed that you are so quickly deserting Him who called you by the grace of Christ, for a different gospel; which is really not another; only there are some who are disturbing you and want to distort the gospel of Christ. But even if we, or an angel from heaven, should preach to you a gospel contrary to what we have preached to you, he is to be accursed! As we have said before so I say again, now, if any man is preaching to you a gospel contrary to what you received, he is to be accursed!*" (*all quotes Ryrie Study Bible NAS*)

Proverbs 30:5-6 states "Every word of God is pure: He is a shield unto them that put their trust in Him. Add thou not unto His words, lest He reprove thee, and thou be found a liar." Proverbs 13:13 states, "Whoso despiseth the Word shall be destroyed; but he that fears the commandment shall be rewarded." Matthew 24:35 states, "Heaven and earth shall pass away, but my words shall not pass away." These verses show the authority of God's Word, the Bible, that it is unchangeable and there are severe penalties if someone adds to it or mocks it.

Christians believe that the Bible is authoritative and meaningful to their lives.

Christians believe that the Bible is the complete Word of God given to mankind for guidance into heaven and for education in Christianity to be lived out here on this temporal plane. I refer you to the Frequently Asked Question XII on The Importance of God's Word and the topical section on "Scripture" in the companion volume of this Christianity series for further insight.

First and foremost, if anyone comes to you saying that God's Word has errors that had to be corrected by them or that some person has special revelations that complete God's Word you can be assured, they are not leading you to God's salvation through Christ or His life of fulfillment and peace. If they ask you to read their book and pray about whether it should be believed, do not accept their challenge. We are never to pray about whether something is true or not, we are to search Scripture (the Bible) and see if it fits what God has told us. When Paul and Silas came to Berea, the people "searched the Scriptures daily" to see if what Paul and Silas were preaching was true. The Word of God (Hebrew Old Testament scrolls at that time) was the standard the Bereans appealed to, not their emotions. Paul in 1 Thessalonians 5:21 says "Prove all things, hold fast that which is good..." James in James 1:6 states "if any of you lack wisdom, let him ask of God that giveth to all men liberally. "Wisdom" in this verse is the Greek word Sophia, not Gnosis which is the term for knowledge. The Bible does not contradict itself but does tell us that God's revealed Word is the final authority, not our feelings, or prayers, no matter how strong those feelings or how sincere those prayers. We are to live in the world according to Scripture, not according to feelings. Jeremiah 17:9 states "The heart is deceitful above all things and desperately wicked: who can know it?" The Bible provides us with an unchanging standard by which our feelings must be measured, not the other way around.

Another issue regarding cults is their view of God and the Trinity. Deuteronomy 6:4 states: "Hear, O-Israel; The LORD our God is one LORD." This is the heart and soul of Judaism – it is monotheism – one God. Isaiah 43:10-11 says "You are my witnesses, saith the LORD, and my servant whom I have chosen: that ye may know and believe me, and understand that I am he: before me there was no God formed, neither shall there be after me. I, even, I, am the LORD; and beside me there is no savior." The Christian finds firm ground in this verse to take a stand. There is only one true God and only that God has offered salvation through His son Jesus Christ. We are not to worship false gods.

God the Father, God the Son and God the Holy Spirit are one entity that we call the Trinity. Although not found in Scripture the descriptive term correctly represents the facts found in Scripture. They are not separate distinct beings but three parts of the same God. In Scripture, God has provided glimpses of Himself by sharing His Names which provide insight into who He is, as you will note in the section here detailing the Names of God in Scripture. One of many connections between the Names of God that show that these Names are for a single being can be found in 1 Kings 18:39; "And when all the people saw it, they fell on their faces: and they said, The LORD (Jehovah), he is the God (Elohim), the LORD (Jehovah), he is the God (Elohim). In Deut 4:35 it says there is none other beside Him, not "them" which is what it would have said if Jehovah (LORD) and Elohim (God) were different beings. Therefore, God the Father, God the Son and God the Holy Spirit created the earth, created mankind and will set in judgment of the world.

Each of the three parts of the Godhead (which Christian's call "The Trinity") have the attributes of deity including Omnipresence (present everywhere at the same point in time Ps 139:7, Jer 23:23-24, Matt 28:20), Omniscience (all-knowing, Ps 147:5, John 16:30; 1 Cor 2:10-11), Omnipotence (all-powerful, Jer 32:17; John 2:1-11; Rom 15:19) and Eternality (Eternal from all time, Ps 90:2; Heb 9:14; Rev 22:13). Scripture teaches that there is three-in-oneness in the Godhead (Matt 28:19, 2 Cor 13:14). Neither Jesus Christ or the Holy Spirit are created entities.

Numbers 23:19 "God is not a man that He should lie; neither the son of man, that He should repent: hath He said shall He not do it? Or hath He spoken, and shall He not make good?" God is not a man, not even an exalted man. God is a completely different order of being than

121

man. Man is God's creation just as Satan, Michael the Archangel, and all other angels were created by the Triune God. In Genesis 6:6 God expresses his deep sorrow at the wickedness of man. God is omnipresent and unlimited and has revealed Himself in the Bible.

So, we see that these cults discount and marginalize Scripture as being the Word of God. They dilute or ignore who God is and what He has done. Additionally, therefore, they must also assault Christ and His redemptive life, death, and resurrection. Paul in his letter to Colossians 1:15-17, speaking of Christ, states "Who is the image of the invisible God, the firstborn of every creature: For by him were all things created, that are in heaven, and that are in the earth, visible and invisible, whether they be thrones, or dominions, or principalities, or powers: all things were created by Him, and for Him: and he is before all things, and by him all things consist." Christ is not just about this earth but also about heaven and all creation. Revelation 22:13 records Christ stating, "I am Alpha and Omega, the beginning and the end, the first and the last." This statement by Christ Himself shows that Christ Jesus is supreme. He is not one of many gods but is the One True God. In Revelation 3:14b He states he is the original, that He is the Ruler of the creation of God.

The sham religions must also downplay or ignore Christ's sacrificial death on the cross for the sin of mankind. The Christian believes that the sacrifice of Jesus Christ is all-powerful and all-sufficient. There is no trespass, no sin, no in-fraction that is so serious that the blood of Jesus Christ is not powerful enough to cleanse it. There is no other means for the salvation of mankind except to accept Christ's death and resurrection. The only unpardonable sin is to reject Christ's death and resurrection. The Holy Spirit convicts us of sin and separation from God. You will not ask for salvation if you have made a decision that you are not a sinner separated from God. To die in that state of denial is the unpardonable sin – dying without accepting Christ's redemptive work for your personal sinfulness. The unpardonable sin is not some level of severity of sin but simply not accepting Christ's offer of salvation.

If there isn't an omnipotent, omnipresent God that exists, if there are instead multiple gods, if man is on the same level as God Himself then there really isn't a literal Hell. Simply in order to justify their marginalization of the Word of God and their lack of anything better to replace it, these sham religions must destroy 1) the idea of God's judgment of man's sin, 2) that there is a literal hell and 3) that there is the possibility of an eternity separated from anything good which involves eternal pain and suffering.

Because we have an eternal soul, we are therefore an eternal being that will live on after death on earth (Gen 35:18, Rev 6:9-10). The Bible shows that unbelievers are conscious in Hell (Matt 13:42, 25:41-46; Luke 16:22:24; Rev 14:11) as are believers in heaven (1 Cor 2:9; 2 Cor 5:6-

8; Phil 1:21-23; Rev 7:17; 21:4). The Bible clearly teaches that Hell is a real place of conscious and eternal suffering (Matt 5:22; 25:41,46; Jude 7; Rev 14:11; 20:10,14).

This life is not a game show where we have multiple doors to choose from for the afterlife. The Bible clearly states that acceptance of Jesus as your personal savior is the ONLY way to enter into God's heaven (John 14:6, Matt 7:13-14, Acts 4:12) and rejection of that "door" has only one result: everlasting torment.

Although there are many other issues involved in the difference between true Christianity and those that try to hide behind it under a veil of religion, these are key points in knowing when something you are being asked or led to believe is false. No matter what you are told or asked to read, search the Scriptures themselves in an internationally respected translation and find the answers yourself.

Reading through the Bible

There are several different options for reading through the Bible noted here. There are many more available online. You can begin those at any date and read through as noted until you have come back to your starting date. You do not have to wait to start on January 1st. It is a good idea to read through the entire Bible so you can grasp the picture and substance of the Book. Topical studies are important for a deeper understanding of situations. They can provide guidance on certain questions you may have or as a study into a particular person and how they related to God.

In the spiritual exercise of reading and studying Scripture, it is important to let God speak to you. The quantity of material you read today is not as important as the quality of what you get out of those verses. Even a person who does not consider themselves to be a "Christian" can ask God to speak to them through the Bible. After reading a passage ask the Holy Spirit to help you see what you need from that passage for that very day. Re-read the passage if necessary, to grasp the meaning. Ask yourself questions about what you have read such as:

- ✓ Does this tell me anything about God or Christ or the Holy Spirit? If so, what?
- ✓ Does this tell me anything about myself and how I should live? If so, what?
- ✓ Does this tell me anything about other people and my responsibilities to, or relationships with them? If so, what?

Keep a journal of your studies and of your prayers (sample on page 7). Write down what this passage meant to you today and your prayer requests to God about today's reading. This will help you to recognize answered prayers in the future. It will help you to see how you have grown in your knowledge and understanding of Christ in the years to come.

Looking online you can find multiple different ways to read through the Bible. You can work straight through, read by chapters, read a mix of New and Old Testament passages each day, read every day, read twice a day, read five days a week, and many other options. It is imperative, though, that you read through the entire Bible every so often so the full spectrum of the Bible can be seen. The methods attached here are examples to get started. The method does not matter; it is the absolute necessity of every Christian to know who God is and who you are in relationship to Him. The only way to do this is by reading the Word of God consistently. If you get behind in a program you have chosen, then change the amount being read or change to another method.
Do Not Stop.Keep going, every day, every month, every year.

Reading Proverbs Daily:

The format in Proverbs lends itself well to read one chapter per day which can be done in excess of the daily portions you might choose for reading through the entire Bible or specific studies.

Reading the Bible through in 88 days

Remember, this is a reading program to get an overview of scripture. Keep a pad and paper handy to write down questions or observations you want to go back afterward to do more research on as well as verses that you want to remember.

Day 1: Gen 1:1- Gen16:16

Day 2: Gen 17:1- Gen 28:22

Day 3: Gen 29:1- Gen 39:23

Day 4: Gen 40:1- Gen 50:26

Day 5: Ex 1:1 – Ex 14:31

Day 6: Ex 15;1 – Ex 28:43

Day 7: Ex 29:1 – Ex 40: 38

Day 8: Lev 1:1 – Lev 14:32

Day 9: Lev 14:33 – Lev 26:13

Day 10: Lev 26:14 – Num 8:4

Day 11: Num 8:5 – Num 20:29

Day 12: Num 21:1 – Num 31:54

Day 13: Num 32:1 – Deut 6:25

Day 14: Deut 7:1 – Deut 22:30

Day 15: Deut 23:1 – Deut 34:12

Day 16: Josh 1:1 – Josh 13:33

Day 17: Josh 14:1 – Judges 3:6

Day 18: Judges 3:7 – Judges 14:20

Day 19: Judges 15:1 – 1 Sam 2:36

Day 20: 1 Sam 3:1 – 1 Sam 15:35

Day 21: 1 Sam 16:1 – 1 Sam 27:12

Day 22: 1 Sam 28:1 – 2 Sam 11:27

Day 23: 2 Sam 12:1 – 2 Sam 21:22

Day 24: 2 Sam 22:1 – 1 Kng 7:12

Day 25: 1 Kng 7:13 –
1 Kng 16:7
Day 26: 1 Kng 16:8 –
2 Kng 4:37
Day 27: 2 Kng 4:38 –
2 Kng 15:22
Day 28: 2 Kng 15:23
– 2 Kng 25:30
Day 29: 1 Chr 1:1 –
1 Chr 9:34
Day 30: 1 Chr 9:35 –
1 Chr 23:32
Day 31: 1 Chr 24:1 –
2 Chr 6:42
Day 32: 2 Chr 7:1 –
2 Chr 22:9
Day 33: 2 Chr 22:10
– 2 Chr 34:33
Day 34: 2 Chr 35:1 –
Ezra 10:44
Day 35: Neh 1:1 –
Neh 12:47
Day 36: Neh 13:1 –
Job 7:21
Day 37: Job 8:1 –
Job 24:25
Day 38: Job 25:1 –
Job 42:17
Day 39: Ps 1:1 –
Ps 23:6

Day 40: Ps 24:1 –
Ps 44:26
Day 41: Ps 45:1 –
Ps 68:35
Day 42: Ps 69:1 –
Ps 88: 18
Day 43: Ps 89:1 –
Ps 107:43
Day 44: Ps 108:1 –
Ps 132: 18
Day 45: Ps 133:1 –
Prov 6:35
Day 46: Prov 7:1 –
Prov 19:29
Day 47: Prov 20:1 –
Ecc 1:18
Day 48: Ecc 2:1 –
Song 8:14
Day 49: Isa 1:1 –
Isa 13:22
Day 50: Isa 14:1 –
Isa 28:29
Day 51: Isa 29:1 –
Isa 40:31
Day: 52: Isa 41:1 –
Isa 51:23
Day 53: Isa 52:1 –
Isa 66:24
Day 54: Jer 1:1 –
Jer 9:26

Day 55: Jer 10:1 –
   Jer 22:30
Day 56 Jer 23:1 –
   Jer 32:44
Day 57: Jer 33:1 –
   Jer 47: 7
Day 58: Jer 48:1 –
   Jer 52:34
Day 59: Lam 1:1 –
   Eze 11:25
Day 60: Eze 12:1 –
   Eze 23:49
Day 61: Eze 24:1 –
   Eze 34:31
Day 62: Eze 35:1 –
   Eze 46:24
Day 63: Eze 47:1 –
   Dan 8:27
Day 64: Dan 9:1 –
   Hos 12:14
Day 65: Hos 13:1 –
   Amos 9:15
Day 66: Oba 1:1 –
   Nah 3: 19
Day 67: Hab 1:1 –
   Zec 9:17
Day 68: Zec 10:1 –
   Matt 4:25
Day 69: Matt 5:1 –
   Matt 15:39

Day 70: Matt 16:1 –
   Matt 26:56
Day 71: Matt 26:57 –
   Mrk 9:1
Day 72: Mrk 8:2 –
   Luke 1:80
Day 73: Luke 2:1 –
   Luke 9:62
Day 74: Luke 10:1 –
   Luke 19:48
Day 75: Luke 20:1 –
   John 5:47
Day 76: John 6:1 –
   John 14:31
Day 77: John 15:1 –
   Acts 5:42
Day 78: Acts 6:1 –
   Acts 16:15
Day 79: Acts 16:16 –
   Acts 28:31
Day 80: Rom 1:1 –
   Rom 13:14
Day 81: Rom 14:1 –
   1 Cor 14:40
Day 82: 1 Cor 15:1 –
   Gal 2:21
Day 83: Gal 3:1 –
   Col 4:18
Day 84: 1 Thess 1:1 –
   Phil 25

Day 85: Heb 1:1 –
Heb 13:25
Day 86: James 1:1 –
3 John 14
Day 87: Jude 1 –
Rev 16:21
Day 88: Rev 17:1 –
Rev 22:21

A Chronological Reading Plan

Adapted from How to Read the Bible Chronologically.
Copyright © 2019.
https://www.thenivbible.com/blog/read-bible-chronologically/

"Reading the Bible chronologically can be a refreshing way to see it through new eyes. We might think that because the Bible starts with creation and ends with Revelation it's already laid out sequentially, but it's not. Reading it in the order that events occurred can equip us to understand its narrative more clearly and see it from a fresh perspective.

It's important to remember that the Bible is a collection of writings. No one sat down and said, "Let's write the Bible from start to finish." The scrolls that make up the books of the Bible were written by more than 30 authors and accumulated over thousands of years.

At the beginning, the Bible is in chronological order. If you read the books of Moses in the order that they appear, you're reading biblical history in its proper sequence. And of course, the Old Testament is chronologically before the New Testament. But eventually, you'll come to places where timelines weave together or overlap. And there is benefit to this arrangement, as for example stopping to read a prophet can give you insight into a historical narrative and reading one of Paul's epistles can clarify events in the story of Acts.

If you are wondering where to get started reading the Bible chronologically, you can purchase the <u>NIV Once-A-Day Bible: Chronological Edition</u> which breaks up the Bible into 365 sequential readings." BlueLetter Bible.org has a one-year reading plan as follows:

Blue Letter Bible *Daily Bible Reading Program*

Chronological Plan

1-Year Plan. These readings are compiled according to recent historical research, considering the order in which the recorded events actually occurred. This is a fantastic plan to follow if you wish to add historical context to your reading of the Bible. If the schedule provided is followed, the entire Bible will be read in one calendar year.

1. Genesis 1-3	14. Job 38-39
2. Genesis 4-7	15. Job 40-42
3. Genesis 8-11	16. Genesis 12-15
4. Job 1-5	17. Genesis 16-18
5. Job 6-9	18. Genesis 19-21
6. Job 10-13	19. Genesis 22-24
7. Job 14-16	20. Genesis 25-26
8. Job 17-20	21. Genesis 27-29
9. Job 21-23	22. Genesis 30-31
10. Job 24-28	23. Genesis 32-34
11. Job 29-31	24. Genesis 35-37
12. Job 32-34	25. Genesis 38-40
13. Job 35-37	26. Genesis 41-42

126. Ps 89, 96, 100-101, 105, 132
127. 2 Samuel 6-7; 1 Chron 17
128. Psalms 25, 29, 33, 36, 39
129. 2 Samuel 8-9; 1 Chron 18
130. Psalms 50, 53, 60, 75
131. 2 Sam 10; 1 Chron 19; Ps 20
132. Psalms 65-67, 69-70
133. 2 Samuel 11-12; 1 Chron 20
134. Psalms 32, 51, 86, 122
135. 2 Samuel 13-15
136. Psalms 3-4, 12-13, 28, 55
137. 2 Samuel 16-18
138. Psalms 26, 40, 58, 61-62, 64
139. 2 Samuel 19-21
140. Psalms 5, 38, 41-42
141. 2 Samuel 22-23; Psalm 57

142. Psalms 95, 97-99
143. 2Sam 24;1Chron 21-22;Ps 30
144. Psalms 108-110
145. 1 Chronicles 23-25
146. Ps 131, 138-139, 143-145
147. 1 Chron 26-29; Psalm 127
148. Psalms 111-118
149. 1 Kings 1-2; Ps 37, 71, 94
150. Psalm 119
151. 1 Kings 3-4
152. 2 Chronicles 1; Psalm 72
153. Song of Solomon
154. Proverbs 1-3
155. Proverbs 4-6
156. Proverbs 7-9
157. Proverbs 10-12
158. Proverbs 13-15
159. Proverbs 16-18
160. Proverbs 19-21
161. Proverbs 22-24
162. 1 Kings 5-6; 2 Chron 2-3

163. 1 Kings 7;
    2 Chronicles 4
164. 1 Kings 8;
    2 Chronicles 5
165. 2 Chronicles 6-7
    Psalm 136
166. Psalms 134,
    146-150
167. 1 Kings 9; 2
    Chronicles 8
168. Proverbs 25-26
169. Proverbs 27-29
170. Ecclesiastes 1-6
171. Ecclesiastes 7-12
172. 1 Kings 10-11;
    2 Chron 9
173. Proverbs 30-31
174. 1 Kings 12-14
175. 2 Chronicles 10-12
176. 1 Kings 15; 2
    Chron 13-16
177. 1 Kings 16; 2
    Chronicles 17
178. 1 Kings 17-19
179. 1 Kings 20-21
180. 1 Kings 22; 2
    Chronicles 18
181. 2 Chronicles 19-23

182. Obadiah;
    Psalms 82-83
183. 2 Kings 1-4
184. 2 Kings 5-8
185. 2 Kings 9-11
186. 2 Kings 12-13;
    2 Chronicles 24
187. 2 Kings 14;
    2 Chronicles 25
188. Jonah
189. 2 Kings 15;
    2 Chronicles 26
190. Isaiah 1-4
191. Isaiah 5-8
192. Amos 1-5
193. Amos 6-9
194. 2 Chronicles 27;
    Isaiah 9-12
195. Micah
196. 2 Chron 28; 2
    Kings 16-17
197. Isaiah 13-17
198. Isaiah 18-22
199. Isaiah 23-27
200. 2 Kgs 18;
    2 Chron 29-31;Ps48
201. Hosea 1-7
202. Hosea 8-14
203. Isaiah 28-30

257. Daniel 4-6
258. Daniel 7-9
259. Daniel 10-12
260. Ezra 1-3
261. Ezra 4-6;
Psalm 137
262. Haggai
263. Zechariah 1-4
264. Zechariah 5-9
265. Zechariah 10-14
266. Esther 1-5
267. Esther 6-10
268. Ezra 7-10
269. Nehemiah 1-5
270. Nehemiah 6-7
271. Nehemiah 8-10
272. Nehemiah 11-
13; Psalm 126
273. Malachi
274. Luke 1; John 1
275. Matthew 1;
Luke 2
276. Matthew 2
277. Matthew 3; Mark 1;
Luke 3
278. Matthew 4;
Luke 4-5
279. John 2-4

280. Matthew 8;
Mark 2
281. John 5
282. Matthew 12;
Mark 3; Luke 6
283. Matthew 5-7
284. Matthew 9;
Luke 7
285. Matthew 11
286. Luke 11
287. Matthew 13;
Luke 8
288. Mark 4-5
289. Matthew 10
290. Matthew 14;
Mark 6; Luke 9
291. John 6
292. Matthew 15;
Mark 7
293. Matthew 16;
Mark 8
294. Matthew 17;
Mark 9
295. Matthew 18
296. John 7-8
297. John 9-10
298. Luke 10
299. Luke 12-13
300. Luke 14-15

345. Romans 14-16
346. Acts 20-23
347. Acts 24-26
348. Acts 27-28
349. Colossians,
    Philemon
350. Ephesians
351. Philippians
352. 1 Timothy
353. Titus
354. 1 Peter
355. Hebrews 1-6
356. Hebrews 7-10
357. Hebrews 11-13
358. 2 Timothy
359. 2 Peter, Jude
360. 1 John
361. 2, 3 John
362. Revelation 1-5
363. Revelation 6-11
364. Revelation 12-18
365. Revelation 19-22

How Do I Memorize Scripture?

Different people memorize in different ways. Don't believe the old excuse that you simply cannot memorize verses, anyone is able to accomplish that task. When you think about it, you memorize a great deal of information every day. How many phone numbers do you know? How many addresses? Most of us, if we sat down and took the time to do it, could create a long list of names and phone numbers and combinations and codes and so on and so on. Hence, you are able to memorize Scripture if you really want to. That is the key – you must desire it with all your heart and be willing to make the commitment that it takes to get the job done.

Repetition is important in learning. You must devise a system whereby you are able to review your verses on a daily basis. This is not something that will end after a verse is memorized – it will go on for the rest of your life if you really want to keep the verses fresh in your mind. A good system is to keep a master list of all verses memorized, as well as those being worked on. Once a verse is memorized, it is placed on the list and reviewed each day for ten days, a place for a mark being available for each of the days. When the ten-day review is over, it is placed in a category that is reviewed once every week or month.

But how do I memorize the verse? The most effective method involves quotation and writing. Read over the verse three or four times, noting the natural breaks and rhythms. Begin trying to quote from memory, making sure to check your accuracy – you don't want to start off memorizing it incorrectly! Once you can quote it ten times straight with the book, chapter and verse number, take out a sheet of paper and begin to write it. Check the written verse for correctness. Write it again and check it again. Write it at least 5 times. This seems to really ingrain the verse in the memory. Make sure to review it each day for at least 10 days.

Once you begin to have a fairly extensive list, you may want to upgrade your system like going to a 3 X 5 card system or a smaller blank business card size. Write the full verse on one side and just the book, chapter and verse number on the other side. This is especially handy in reviewing a long list of verses. It is also helpful to be able to categorize the verses in general category headings.

There are numerous variations on the above method. No matter how you do it, make it a priority. Without a commitment to following through you will never get the verses down. Believe me, the thrill of being able to answer the non-believer's questions while pushing forward the claims of Christ on their lives is well worth the effort of memorization.

.

Steps to Peace With God

1. God's Purpose: Peace and Life

God loves you and wants you to experience peace and life—abundant and eternal.

The Bible Says ...

"We have peace with God through our Lord Jesus Christ." *Romans 5:1, NKJV*

"For God so loved the world that He gave His only begotten Son, that whoever believes in Him should not perish but have everlasting life." *John 3:16, NKJV*

"I have come that they may have life, and that they may have it more abundantly." *John 10:10, NKJV*

Since God planned for us to have peace and the abundant life right now, why are most people not having this experience?

2. Our Problem: Separation From God

God created us in His own image to have an abundant life. He did not make us as robots to automatically love and obey Him, but gave us a will and a freedom of choice.

We chose to disobey God and go our own willful way. We still make this choice today. This results in separation from God.

The Bible Says ...

"For all have sinned and fall short of the glory of God." *Romans 3:23, NKJV*

"For the wages of sin is death, but the gift of God is eternal life in Christ Jesus our Lord." *Romans 6:23, NKJV*

Our choice results in separation from God.

People (Sinful)   **God (Holy)**

143

OUR ATTEMPTS

Through the ages, individuals have tried in many ways to bridge this gap ... without success ...

THE BIBLE SAYS ...

"There is a way that seems right to a man, but its end is the way of death."
Proverbs 14:12, NKJV

"But your iniquities have separated you from your God; and your sins have hidden His face from you, so that He will not hear."
Isaiah 59:2, NKJV

There is only one remedy for this problem of separation.

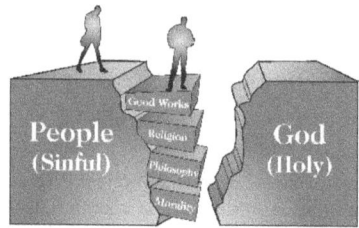

People (Sinful)   Good Works   God (Holy)
Religion
Philosophy
Morality

3. GOD'S REMEDY: THE CROSS

Jesus Christ is the only answer to this problem. He died on the cross and rose from the grave, paying the penalty for our sin and bridging the gap between God and people.

THE BIBLE SAYS ...

"For there is one God and one Mediator between God and men, the Man Christ Jesus."
1 Timothy 2:5, NKJV

"For Christ also suffered once for sins, the just for the unjust, that He might bring us to God."
1 Peter 3:18, NKJV

"But God shows his love for us in that while we were still sinners, Christ died for us." *Romans 5:8, ESV*

God has provided the only way ... we must make the choice ...

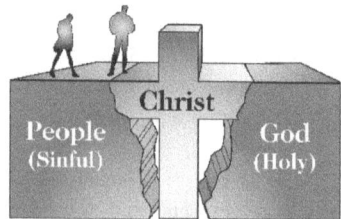

People (Sinful)   Christ   God (Holy)

4. Our Response: Receive Christ

We must trust Jesus Christ and receive Him by personal invitation.

The Bible Says ...

"Behold, I stand at the door and knock. If anyone hears My voice and opens the door, I will come in to him and dine with him, and he with Me." *Revelation 3:20, NKJV*

"But to all who did receive him, who believed in his name, he gave the right to become children of God." *John 1:12, ESV*

"If you confess with your mouth that Jesus is Lord and believe in your heart that God raised him from the dead, you will be saved." *Romans 10:9, ESV*

Are you here ... or here?

People
Sin
Rebellion
Separation

Christ

God
Peace
Forgiveness
Abundant Life
Eternal Life

Is there any good reason why you cannot receive Jesus Christ right now?

How to Receive Christ:

1. Admit your need (say, "I am a sinner").
2. Be willing to turn from your sins (repent) and ask for God's forgiveness.
3. Believe that Jesus Christ died for you on the cross and rose from the grave.
4. Through prayer, invite Jesus Christ to come in and control your life through the Holy Spirit (receive Jesus as Lord and Savior).

What to Pray:

Dear God,
    I know that I am a sinner. I want to turn from my sins, and I ask for Your forgiveness. I believe that Jesus Christ is Your Son. I believe He died for my sins and that You raised Him to life. I want Him to come into my heart and to take control of my life. I want to trust Jesus as my Savior and follow Him as my Lord from this day forward.

In Jesus' Name, amen.

_____   _____
Date   Signature

God's Assurance: His Word

If you prayed this prayer,

the Bible says ...

"For 'everyone who calls on the name of the Lord will be saved.'" *Romans 10:13, ESV*

Did you sincerely ask Jesus Christ to come into your life? Where is He right now? What has He given you?

"For by grace you have been saved through faith. And this is not your own doing; it is the gift of God, not a result of works, so that no one may boast." *Ephesians 2:8–9, ESV*

the Bible says ...

"He who has the Son has life; he who does not have the Son of God does not have life. These things I have written to you who believe in the name of the Son of God, that you may know that you have eternal life, and that you may continue to believe in the name of the Son of God." *1 John 5:12–13, NKJV*

Receiving Christ, we are born into God's family through the supernatural work of the Holy Spirit, who indwells every believer. This is called regeneration or the "new birth."

This is just the beginning of a wonderful new life in Christ. To deepen this relationship you should:

1. Read your Bible every day to know Christ better.
2. Talk to God in prayer every day.
3. Tell others about Christ.
4. Worship, fellowship, and serve with other Christians in a church where Christ is preached.
5. As Christ's representative in a needy world, demonstrate your new life by your love and concern for others.

God bless you as you do.

Franklin Graham

If you want further help in the decision you have made, write to:
Billy Graham Evangelistic Association
1 Billy Graham Parkway, Charlotte, NC 28201-0001

1-877-2GRAHAM (1-877-247-2426)
BillyGraham.org/commitment

NOTES:

See FAQ Section

The Escalator to Depression:

Psalm 42:1 5 is a Psalm of Depression, could not sleep, eat, felt lonely

Verse 5: Question – Introspection – Why am I going through this depression?

Answer ---- Hope in God – Turn your attention away from yourself and focus on God

Examples of Depression:

Common to all was an improper response to a life situation

1 Kings 19:1-4	Elijah	V3 = fear
Gen 4:3-7	Cain	V 5,6 = anger
Numb 11:10-15	Moses	
Jonah 4:1 10	Jonah	

Jezebel rejected him

God rejected his offering and Cain took it personally self pity

He was disappointed when the nation repented

4: Appropriate it by faith
3: Know God's promises
2: Know who you are in Christ
1: Know who Christ is.

Death to Self

Our natural incorrect response to a life situation:

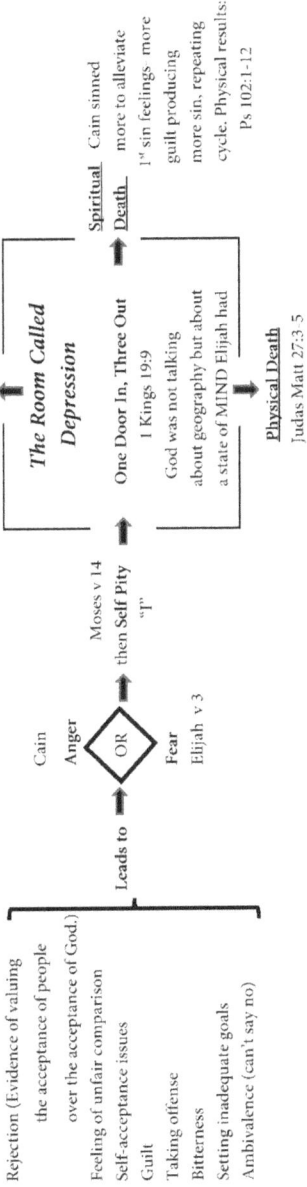

Rejection (Evidence of valuing the acceptance of people over the acceptance of God.)
Feeling of unfair comparison
Self-acceptance issues
Guilt
Taking offense
Bitterness
Setting inadequate goals
Ambivalence (can't say no)

Leads to → OR

Cain
Anger

Moses v 14
then Self Pity
"I"

Fear
Elijah v 3

The Room Called Depression

One Door In, Three Out
1 Kings 19:9
God was not talking about geography but about a state of MIND Elijah had

Physical Death
Judas Matt 27:3 5

Spiritual **Death** Cain sinned more to alleviate 1st sin feelings more guilt producing more sin, repeating cycle. Physical results: Ps 102:1-12

NOTES:

The Fountain of True Success

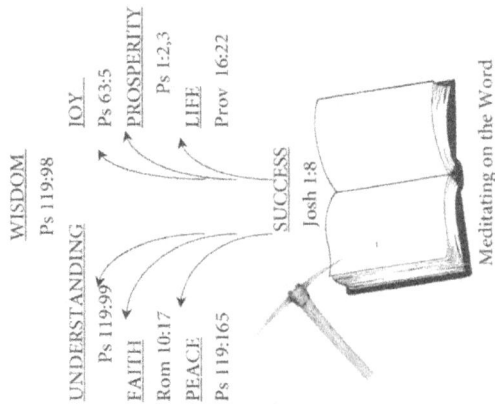

WISDOM
Ps 119:98

JOY
Ps 63:5

UNDERSTANDING
Ps 119:99

PROSPERITY
Ps 1:2,3

FAITH
Rom 10:17

LIFE
Prov 16:22

PEACE
Ps 119:165

SUCCESS
Josh 1:8

Meditating on the Word

Christian Cycle of Life

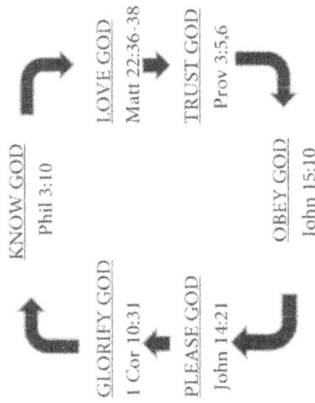

KNOW GOD
Phil 3:10

LOVE GOD
Matt 22:36-38

TRUST GOD
Prov 3:5,6

GLORIFY GOD
1 Cor 10:31

PLEASE GOD
John 14:21

OBEY GOD
John 15:10

Finances:

1: God is the source
   Matt 5:31,32
   Phil 4:19
2: Giving
   Luke 6:38
   Prov 3:9,10
   Deut 14:23 (c)
3. Saving
   Example Joseph for famine
   Prov 21:20
4. Avoid get-rich-quick schemes
   Prov 28:22

www.ingramcontent.com/pod-product-compliance
Lightning Source LLC
Chambersburg PA
CBHW060043030426
42334CB00019B/2472